Under a Full Moon and a Guiding Star

By Lani Almanza

Dedicated to:

In memory of

Jacob Michael Almanza

CT Ticknor and Mel Rice

And to my family:

You have all been guiding stars on my journey.

Dear Reader,

During the writing process, what I saw evolve was that my life has been moving between two main mindsets - Doing and Being or Yin and Yang. These mindsets became the framework for the book. And in between, I have shared a significant experience of transformation which led me further on the journey as a caregiver.

The book title and cover, Under A Full Moon and A Guiding Star, shines a light on that journey.

In order to find and maintain my balance between the Doing and Being, I am committed to a daily practice of wellness. And so throughout the book I have shared images, tools, and resources, such as meditations and visualizations, towards helping you live a healthier and happier life. I hope you connect with the true meaning of ALOHA and trust that I am walking alongside you as an alaka'i (guide in the Hawaiian language), offering the wisdom of having walked the path before. Over my lifetime, I have been fortunate to have a few very special mentors influence my life, and I discovered that is also my gift – to guide and support people through life's journey and transitions. I have built up that skill through personal and professional experiences, which have now become Alaka'i Associates. In gratitude, I invite you to join me on the journey.

Table of Contents

This honu icon - directs you to an Alaka'i Lesson in Part III

PART I: DOING AND BEING

"We are descendants of our ancestors, and ancestors to our descendants." ~ Unknown

---

Generations

As I look back over my life, I have realized that there were guides, alaka'i, if you will, along the way that influenced me and my ability to understand the two ways I have been living: in the doing or in the being. Four of those alaka'i were my grandparents. Their personalities and the lives they chose to lead gave me a glimpse of both ways of living, doing, and being.

My maternal grandmother seemed to be very straight-laced, kept a clean house, and raised two daughters, but what I learned was that her outward appearance was just a cover-up for the spunk and humor she had. My maternal grandfather was just a happy man, who didn't let much upset his demeanor, and while he worked long hours, he found his balance by going fishing, which I was able to experience with him as a young child.

My paternal grandmother was a pint-sized firecracker. All 4 feet 11 inches of her (and maybe that was even in heels). She raised four children in rural Nebraska and was recognized as a pillar of the community (all 411 citizens). She loved to bake, which is a passion she shared with my father that has been passed down to two more generations. Last but not least is my paternal grandfather. He was a tall, solid man, a banker and insurance salesman, but here is my memory that best describes him:

Behind my grandparents' pink-painted stucco house and beyond the screened-in patio was my grandfather's garden. Rows of roses and gladiolus were for my grandmother, and rows of vegetables – corn, tomatoes, green beans, and more. I believe tending his garden was my grandfather's meditation and connection with his creator. Most days, he would come home for lunch and spend a few minutes out there watering or just checking on the plants, and then after work would do some more serious gardening, pulling weeds, hoeing, and harvesting. I recall learning how to shuck corn and snap beans from that garden. And the tomatoes – like nothing you have ever tasted! Firm and full of sun-kissed flavor.

I am certain this is where he communed and conversed with God, so much so that it was in his garden that he took his last breath. He was so connected to that place that on my way back from his memorial service, as I walked into the garden from the back gate, I could still feel his presence and his peace. And it was no wonder that the following was one of his favorite hymns.

In The Garden

I come to the garden alone,

While the dew is still on the roses,

And the voice I hear, falling on my ear,

The Son of God discloses.

And He walks with me, and He talks with me,

And He tells me I am His own,

And the joy we share as we tarry there,

None other has ever known.

The Artist in Me

I was born to a father who was an artist and interior designer. When I turned one, he had completed two years of active duty in the Navy and signed up for four more with the Navy Reserves so that he could attend the Kansas City Art Institute in Kansas City, Missouri. As soon as he graduated, we moved back to Hawai'i, where he began his career. He absolutely loved his work, and eventually, Ronald Kats became a well-known and sought-after designer in Hawaii. Our house became an ongoing showroom as new styles of decor came and went. From blue shag carpets to soft peach tones, from dark hardwoods to light bamboo. Through his eyes, I gained an appreciation for all styles of art and would often pull out one of his books on architecture or artists to understand how he saw the world. I remember when he was selected to create a showroom in the Parade of Homes in Honolulu; he had decided on a white and silver motif and had gone to a thrift store and bought several dozen books to put on the shelves. However, to make it all work with the white and silver theme, he had me help him cover all the books in foil, some with the shiny side facing out and some with the matte part facing out. It turned out to be spectacular. His appreciation for art was not just for the interior, though. He also loved the colors of the natural environment of Hawai'i, especially the greens and blues, from the mountains to the ocean, which he used to connect both interior and exterior design. That gift of seeing the world through someone else's eyes and art was also passed on to my children and now my grandchildren, who express their own unique creative gifts. One is a very talented graphic artist, one is a compassionate communicator, and two are great storytellers.

My father also taught me to value art by giving me some unique and valuable pieces throughout my lifetime, including two original Madge Tennant drawings, a couple of sets of candlesticks from his collection of more than 50, and a collection of first-edition Beatrix Potter books. I am now able to find art in almost all aspects of life. Thanks, Dad.

Mothers

Born to a mother who was a lifelong musician, music has always been part of who I am. Her musical journey began with piano lessons at age five, and then, at age seven she added the violin. By the time she was in college, she was teaching piano to help pay for her tuition. From my earliest recollections of my mother playing violin in the Honolulu Symphony and piano at church, I was exposed to all genres of music - classical, jazz, contemporary, and pop. One of my fond memories was when I was about five or six years old, at the summer concert series at the Waikīkī Shell amphitheater, usually held on a Sunday afternoon. I attended with my father, and the guest artist for this particular concert was one of my parents' favorite singers, Harry Belafonte. Just before intermission, my father and I headed backstage to see my mom, and as we were waiting, Harry came along and engaged in conversation with my dad and then, for whatever reason, lifted me up for a piggyback ride. Those Sunday outings became a standing date with my parents until I was an adult, attending symphony concerts and opera. It was a privilege I enjoyed being the oldest child.

When I turned seven, my mother enrolled me in piano lessons. I loved my piano teacher; she even made the theory of music interesting to a seven-year-old. In fact, I still have my notebook from those lessons. After five years with her, I graduated from her program, but as I was entering my preteen years I became less interested in formal lessons, and I am grateful to my mother for not insisting that I continue. Even though I sometimes wish I had retained some of that skill, it instilled in me a deep connection to music. In intermediate school, I was fortunate to have a choir teacher who encouraged me to use my voice and at one time, I became part of a trio singing at church, then as an adult singing in a church choir and as a cantor.

Another wonderful musical influence was both my parents' love for musical theater. Whether it was live or on TV, for us, it was just more enjoyable when music was involved. The first musical film I remember seeing was Porgy and Bess at age five (1960) in Kansas City, Missouri. As I look back, I was probably too young to understand at the time, but the fact that my Caucasian parents took me to see a movie musical with Black actors about Black people, reflected their progressive and inclusive view of the world.

Of course, growing up in the 60’s and 70’s, rock music greatly influenced my perspective of the world, again for which I am grateful. It allowed me to be open to the music that came after and influenced my children. Music has a universal language and voice that vibrates with our energy and can connect us where words fail. As I am writing this book, my mother made her transition and is now playing with an orchestra of angels—and the music remains in me.

My mother, Donna, was not equipped to be a wife or a mother at first. She had spent her entire life focused on her musical talents with piano and violin, so much so that at the time she got married, she didn’t know how to boil water. Thankfully my father had helped raise his twin sisters and was there to teach her. She worked really hard during the 1960’s and 70's to fill the role of “housewife” while also trying to pursue her passion with music and playing in the symphony. She had learned how to sew, so with my father in the interior design business, she often had fabric left over from an interior design job to create family-matching outfits. She also was entrepreneurial in creating a small business making men’s neckties, and gift cards made with seaweed she collected and pressed onto the stationary. And she was the keeper of the family finances—down to the penny!

I carry my maternal grandmother with me in my middle name, Marie. In the first five years of my life, I spent significant time with her and my grandfather, and then every few years after that, growing up. As the first grandchild, we had a special bond that gave me a sense of order and safety. She kept a meticulous house but also had a great sense of humor. I remember one summer with her when I was learning to sew and got to use her old Singer foot pedal machine. That memory stuck with me so much so that the one thing I wanted from her estate was her beautiful wooden sewing kit. What I learned about her as a mother was a much more stern picture. I don’t think she felt equipped to be a mother, so she was quite strict with my mother and her sister. I discovered later in life that she had been quite a rebel—being the next to the youngest of eight children. In the 1920’s, when she was in high school, she played basketball. Back then, the uniforms were dresses with socks that went ALL the way up over your knees. (The less flesh showing, the better!) Well, Marie convinced her teammates to roll down their socks right before leaving the locker room and created quite a shock as they came out on the court exposing those KNEES! I really liked learning about her, and it seemed to explain why my mother left

Nebraska to travel to Hawai'i to marry a man that her mother wasn't really sure about as her marriage itself had a little bit of rebellion.

My paternal grandmother, Erma, was a petite little fire plug, who at all of 4 foot 11 inches, was absolutely the boss of the house. She taught me how to bake and play gin rummy, among other things. She was born, raised, and raised her family in rural Nebraska. In her late 30's she was pregnant with my twin aunts and developed rheumatoid arthritis. My father, being 13 years old at the time, became her "right-hand man," helping to cook, clean, and care for the twins. But she never lost her spunk. I recall once when my grandfather had been out with the men, and she knew he would have smoked a cigar, met him at the back door of the house to tell him he needed to remove his clothes and wash up before coming up for dinner. Smoking, and even the smell of smoke, was not allowed in her house! Since my grandfather was a respected leader in the town, my grandmother was always well-dressed and well-coiffed. She had a standing appointment with the beauty parlor down the street once a week. I also spent a lot of time with her as a young child, and over the years, came to appreciate her lessons of strength and endurance.

As I look at my own mothering, I can see that both my grandmothers and my mother have influenced who I have become; however, I have so much more to grow into, even now as I move from mother to grandmother. And I reflect on how I have influenced my daughter and now granddaughters in a mother role they might take on. It is a privilege, a kuleana (responsibility), and it requires me to live ALOHA.

Looking back, who were the family members that were there to guide you? How can you express your gratitude for their presence in your life?

Where I Come From

"Our cultural identities are…always in a state of becoming, a journey in which we never arrive…" ~ *Heneriko, 1994*

In the 1960's, I lived in a neighborhood in Kailua, Hawaii, where every house had a front lawn and life revolved around schedules. Television was a new technology, and kids played with Davy Crockett hats. The future was going to be full of surprises. But I also recall in second grade having air-raid drills where we all hid under our desks or filed out behind the building to kneel down with our heads between our knees and arms over our head while the sirens blared the warning signals. And then there was the assassination of President John F. Kennedy. All I really knew at the time was that he was about my father's age, had a family, and was the President of the United States. Yet that was enough to make an impression on this eight-year-old. Another defining moment was the summer of 1969 while visiting my aunt in Nebraska, witnessing the phenomenon of men walking on the moon.

As a child, I wasn't aware of the extent to which I was being programmed by print and television. Between the 6 o'clock news and the teen magazines, my identity as an American girl was being manufactured for me. It wasn't until my forties, when I read *Manufacturing Consent* by Noam Chomsky that I became aware of how insidious that media influence was in shaping my identity. And it still is. Throughout my lifetime, I have been identified as

American, Caucasian, daughter, granddaughter, friend, sister, student, teenager, wife, mother, employee, teacher, employer, administrator, trainer, and woman. And yet those are roles and never really define who I am. As an adult, I have come to the awareness that I am so much more than any of these roles. I am of the land of my birth, a kama'āina.

While I was growing up in that rural neighborhood on the island of O'ahu in Hawai'i, there began a resurgence of the indigenous Hawaiian identity that had almost been obliterated by colonization. The traditional music, dance, and social structure of the Hawaiians became a focus in education and the arts. Many of us welcomed this as it felt like the right thing to do. But not for all. Being Hawaiian is an ethnic determiner, yet if you were born and raised in Hawaii, you are considered kama'āina. Kama'āina describes Hawai'i residents regardless of their racial background, as opposed to kanaka, which means a person of Native Hawaiian ancestry. While I am Caucasian, I have always considered myself to be kama'āina. The term haole is a Hawaiian word that generally means white or Caucasian, but it can also refer to someone who is an outsider and represents a colonialistic perspective. I never identified with "haole" in a derogatory sense, but at the same time, I recall that I would occasionally define other Caucasian children as the "white haole." This separation was created between those who were born and raised in Hawaii versus those who moved to Hawaii from the continental U.S. and were often teased as outsiders. It wasn't until later that I understood why that distinction made a difference.

As an adult, I began to explore my own racial awareness, and I realized that it came with a certain privilege. Being a "privileged, white female" meant that I was able to live comfortably with food, shelter, clothing, and support. However, being raised in rural O'ahu in the 1960's–70's, I was exposed to friends that were not white and not so privileged. For instance, many of my Caucasian friends had nice homes or cars when many of my local friends did not. I believe this had a significant impact on how I viewed the world. I wanted to include those different or with less into my circle of privilege. One way I accommodated this was to become proficient in pidgin English, which is akin to Creole, a blend of immigrant languages that formed a common bond. This was our means of communication outside the classroom or home. It created a commonality whereby we could be friends beyond those prescribed divisions. It made me grateful for my parents, who did not try to deny their racial identity of being Caucasian, and at the same time, had the courage to step beyond the boundaries of "middle America" Nebraska to settle in Hawaii to raise children with a respect for cultural diversity and acceptance of others on their virtue as individuals, first and foremost. I recognize that each person engages in this struggle for themselves, and in that way, we are all connected. We are all so much more.

ALOHA

I learned the value of our aloha culture through connections with family, friends, neighbors, church, school, teachers, and mentors. I didn't understand it when I was younger the way I do now, but because it was integrated into how I was raised, it became a foundation for my core values.

I was blessed that the Universe/God/ Source/Creator guided my parents from Nebraska to Hawai'i so that I can call it my home. Hawai'i is a special place because of

ALOHA, as defined by Pilahi Paki…

A – Akahai – meaning Kindness to be expressed with a feeling of tenderness

L – Lōkahi – meaning Unity to be expressed with a feeling of harmony

O – 'Olu'olu – meaning Agreeable to be expressed with a feeling of pleasantness

H – Ha'aha'a – meaning Humility to be expressed with a feeling of modesty

A – Ahonui – meaning Patience to be applied with perseverance

(reference: ALOHA by Paki)

To truly live aloha, you must employ all five components. One does not exist without the others. The connections of aloha in my life will unfold as we journey together.

Yin & Yang

Now here I am, at 67, writing a book, a story, about the journey of a lifetime! Age and experience allowed me the perspective to look back and see how I found my way and myself. It is my hope and desire that you find connections with your own journey and perhaps a few guideposts to help you along the way. In the writing of this book, I have discovered there is a unique dance between doing and being. Much like yin and yang, there is a little of each in the other. And for one to be defined, the opposite must exist. We are always partners in the mystery.

Sometimes in the mystery, that yin and yang is revealed to us through animals. As I look back on a life of doing and being, there has always been a pet along the way that, while it may have been unnoticed at the time, I now know to have been spirit guides teaching me the lessons of *doing* and *being*. Two such spirits left a significant mark on my life over the years.

Dexter, the Doing Cat

After losing one of our pet cats, we were at the vet, and they happened to have this little black and white kitten for adoption. My youngest son, Jacob, was about seven years old and immediately bonded with this kitten. So, yes, we bring him home, and he is given a name that was a reference to a shy, nerdy kid at his school. Well, Dexter turns out to be the opposite of shy; he has no fear. He would chase down a dog five times his size and take on any other cat despite the fact that he was often not the victor. One such incident left him with a rather large gash on his head, and he had to have half of his head shaved to clean it and stitch it. He looked a bit strange to say the least. At that time, we happened to be having a private security company watch our house, and one day, while the security watch guy was parked in our front yard, minding his own business, Dexter jumped up on the hood of the car like he's ready to take on this intruder and nearly scares the *&^% out of the guy. He said he thought he was being attacked by "RoboCat."

Another adventure with Dexter was during Christmas. We had some lights on the outside of our kitchen window that were plugged in through the screen to our kitchen counter. Dexter must have thought it looked like a lizard because he decided to jump up on the counter and bite it. Well, he bit through to the wires, which gave him a shock—like the one you see in the movie or cartoons, where the cat's hair stands on end! He ran around the house until we opened a door for him, and when he returned, he had a perpetual drool, which made him all that much more endearing but always in the "doing."

Caspar, the Being Cat

Many years later, our daughter comes home from school with a small bundle covered with fleas and says her teacher found it and asked if anyone could adopt it. So she says yes, despite the fact that we already had at least two other cats in the house at the time. After a good bath, and as I was drying him off, those two cats were very curious to see what was making the noise in the towel. As they came closer, this little white puff of fur popped out, and the two of them ran off scared. So Caspar (the friendly ghost) became his name. That small white kitten grew into the Zen Master. He was our son Joshua's spirit guide, a quiet source of comfort, and was an angel that stayed by Jacob's side until he transitioned. In Jacob's last few weeks, we witnessed the most amazing blessing with Caspar. Jacob was confined to a hospital bed in our living room, and was in a coma. Caspar would come in and gently jump up on the bed at Jacob's feet, walk quietly to his face, and lean in. Once Jacob had taken a few breaths, he would go back down and lay at his feet. Showing us how to just BE. Be present in the moment, be present with one another. We just knew he was guiding Jacob across the bridge. Caspar's cancer was also progressing at the same time. A year later when he was almost 19 years old, cancer took him across the rainbow bridge. I firmly believe that Jacob has been united with Dexter, Caspar, and all the animal spirit guides that have blessed our family. They are there if you look for them.

When we are able to cultivate the *being* mindset, even in the midst of the *doing*, we can find more ease in our choice of caregiving at any point in our life. In the *being* mindset, there is still some *doing* that needs to take place. This includes being willing to seek guidance and direction from the people and resources that support the being mindset. Finding the balance between the doing of caregiving and the being of caregiving is not an easy task. We may lose sight of the need to stay present to the intrinsic value and reward of caring for others and ourselves, especially when the actions and responsibilities can be so immediate and necessary for the person in need of care.

From Doing to Being as a Caregiver

"I have come to trust not that events will always unfold exactly how I want but that I will be fine either way. The challenges we face in life are always lessons that serve our soul's growth." ~ Marianne Williamson

---

I was the eldest of four children, so by the time I was about ten years old, I became the babysitter for my siblings and then for the neighborhood children as well. I believe this is where my caregiving roots took hold. I didn't know it at the time, but caring for others would become a key factor and kuleana (Hawaiian value of responsibility and privilege) in my life. Looking back, I can see that there are times when I was chosen for a caregiving role and then other times when I chose it.

One of those times is a fond memory of my teenage years with the opportunity to participate in a program called *Candy Stripers,* where teenage girls could volunteer at hospitals as an introduction to the nursing profession, a caregiving role. I loved that experience and still have my uniform 50 years later.

I remember one nurse and a patient experience that really had me considering it as a possible occupation. Our duties as Candy Stripers included going to each patient's room to refresh their water pitcher, provide clean bed table trash bags, and offer reading materials. I had been assigned to the surgical recovery floor with one of my favorite nurses who was a great teacher with a genuinely positive outlook (an example of ALOHA I didn't know at the time). This particular day there was a new patient being admitted who was an exceptionally large man. First, I had to go get him at the check-in downstairs, so off I went with a standard wheelchair. We quickly realized that definitely was not going to work and had to wait for them to find a wider chair to accommodate him. Next, my little 14-year-old self had to push this 300-plus pound man to the elevator and maneuver him in and out and into his room. Whew! Now, in comes the nurse, and she realizes that he is going to need two XXXL gowns, one for the front and one for the back. Her positive and humorous demeanor put us all at ease, and that patient thanked me for my help. That small affirmation has stayed with me all these years so that I can now see that caregiving is part of who I am.

A New Kind of Caregiver

"And every day, the world will drag you by the hand, yelling, "This is important! And this is important! And this is important! You need to worry about this! And this! And this! And each day, it's up to you to yank your hand back, put it on your heart and say, "No. This is what's important." ~ Iain Thomas

---

At the end of my senior year in high school my life had taken a turn towards a new direction in caregiving. Let me share a story with you about One Enchanted Evening. One of my favorite movies is South Pacific and in the song, "Some Enchanted Evening", with one line of lyrics says, "... you may see a stranger across a crowded room..."

I had heard about him from my friends at Kailua High School and their descriptions intrigued me. The girls said he was "tall, dark, and handsome" and the guys said, "He's a really good guy." Well, now I had my chance to see for myself. He was going to be at a graduation party I was attending and besides me having a look I wanted to catch his attention. So, I put on a mesh, flesh-colored pants suit that fit me like a second skin! The party house was bustling, people packing the hallways and stairwells. They littered the floor and the yard. I squeezed my way past them to the backyard because I had heard that's where he was. As my eyes scanned the yard they locked on the stranger amongst a circle of friends. That must be him, definitely tall and lean, brown skin, long wavy black hair; yes, definitely handsome! All of a sudden I feel like I am in one of those romantic movies. His eyes meet mine and I feel my heart jump. Where will this lead?

That enchanted evening led to marriage the following year, and now celebrating 50 years. And, until recently I didn't know his first impression of me was that I looked like Carole King and he might have "felt the earth move."

The early years of married life seemed to move along pretty smoothly. I loved the feeling of independence and adulthood of being married and being a mom. Since I had been caregiving in some way since childhood, I now chose that role for myself. Organizing and managing a household were skills I was good at. Everything from budgeting, paying the bills, cooking, cleaning, sewing; all those domestic skills that I thought defined me, even with the sleepless nights and dirty diapers. And without even realizing it, I was in a new caregiver role again, and again, and again, and again. Yes! Four children by the age of 29! I suppose there were breaks or rest stops along the way, but all that organizing and managing seemed to start running together, life was a constant flurry of doing.

Here's how it looked: **She** is Me

She arrives home from work and school, after picking up her teenage son from basketball practice. **She** puts down her bag and sees the answering machine flashing. **She** retrieves the mail from the mailbox and the groceries from the car as the five cats run interference indicating their immediate need for attention and food. All the while the teenager is posing questions as to how much longer will it take for him to grow to 6', and if his feet grow first does that indicate a growth spurt, and by the way, that means he needs new shoes,like now. **She** kicks off her shoes and heads to the kitchen to unload the groceries, feed the cats, and figure out what to cook for dinner. **She** has done this routine a thousand times. **She** has worked outside the home while also working the "other jobs" of housekeeper, cook, chauffeur, sports team mom, family nurse, and counselor. As dinner cooks there is a brief respite for a glass of iced tea while opening, sorting, and reading the mail. Following dinner **She** asks for the zillionth time for her husband and children to assist with cleaning up. After that there is usually a load of laundry that needs to be done and oh, yeah, homework, you see **She** is also continuing to take classes to complete her degree. Somewhere around 10:30 pm, or later, **She** heads to bed with the prospect of doing it all again tomorrow.

All that organizing and managing compounded until.....

Until the day I was leaving work, with four kids in the car after school, and as I pulled out of the parking lot I saw something fly off the back of my car. Thankfully there were no cars coming and the children were safely secured in the car, but I slammed on the brakes as I realized that it was my datebook/planner, my LIFE, that was in the road!! Every activity, from soccer practices to doctor appointments, plus work and everything else for organizing and managing a family of six was in there! I'm sure many caregivers can relate to that frantic feeling. I think that might have been the moment where I realized that under all the hats I was wearing I had lost my sense of self as Lani — my I AM. That is where I started what I call my archeological dig. This is where I began to realize that I thought it was my role, my job, as an adult, wife, and mother to be always doing for and giving to others. An outward expression of caregiving. But what about the inward expression of caring for self? That wisdom would come later.

But, I knew I had to press the pause button, BIG TIME! One of the first steps I took was to schedule a one-day retreat away from my house, with just me and a journal. Even if all I did was take a nap that day, I just needed to have a chance to breathe. I may not have recognized it at the time but learning to pause and breathe would become a big part of my wellness journey.

And then life stops.....

It was the first day of kindergarten for my youngest child. We were home early so I decided to take on a project in the kitchen and he went to play across the street at the neighbor's house. Around 5pm I called out the kitchen window for him to come home, and at that very moment, as he was coming out of the neighbor's driveway, I heard a car coming up the street. I knew it before I could even get to the doorway. He had been hit. As I ran out the door, I could see that little 5-year-old body lying in the street and remember saying, "Not now, God!" A neighbor stopped me for a second and I was able to gather myself to attend to him. Everything seemed to move in slow motion and the sounds around me seemed distant. He was unconscious and I could tell his leg was probably broken, but I just knelt down and whispered in his ear to come back, it was going to be alright. I moved methodically through all the proper first-aid responses and he regained consciousness but was not fully present and we were rushed off to the hospital. I did not leave his side for the next 24 hours. It wasn't until the hospital said he was in the clear that I went home and cried. He was put in a body cast for three months and so our whole family was thrust into caregiving roles we didn't choose. We all learned how to help him use the bedpan and urinal, how to do a sponge bath, and how to lift a five year old in a full body cast. Thankfully we had the support of our faith community that helped relieve some of those duties so that we could all continue with work and school.

Finding the Being in the Doing

"Everything changed the day she figured out there was exactly enough time for the important things in her life." ~ Brian Andreas

---

Examining sixty-plus years of life experiences takes a lot of consideration! There was a time when my time was all about the *doing* and I really worked hard on managing my time. Over time and through experience that focus has shifted and I have come to understand time in a much more balanced way that is now woven into my daily life.

Since the dawn of humankind we have tried to understand the nature of time. Time has a dual nature that in Greek philosophy are known as chronos and kairos. Most of what we acknowledge in our Western world view as time is the chronos side. The clocks, calendars, agendas, schedules, deadlines.Chronos keeps track of every minute and keeps us running the marathon towards some perceived finish line. Kairos, on the other hand, is the infinite, transcendent, reverent and sacred side. In kairos we can let go of the control.

Chronos is where we are when we are in the *doing* mindset. Chronos is looking for speed and efficiency, where time can seem compressed and slipping through our fingers. It is often described as "spending time." In our efforts to control time we sometimes lose the gift of presence. Kairos is where we are when we are in the *being* mindset. Kairos requires space and allows time to extend and expand. We may not recognize it but we experience kairos when we are in flow with our passion and purpose. This is often described as "valuing time."

So how do we work with this duality? It is much like yin and yang, where there is always a bit of one in the other. Once you are aware of the two sides you can then cultivate ways to create more kairos time in your life.

Here are a few suggestions to begin to find the balance between the two:

- Pause — follow the lesson of breathing. Right there you shifted from chronos to kairos.
- Slow down — follow the lesson of creating "white space" in your schedule.
- Focus – on one task at a time, giving it the care and attention it requires.

By making conscious and consistent decisions to be in kairos you will find that your mind, body, and spirit will prefer to be there more often. Being will come all in good time.

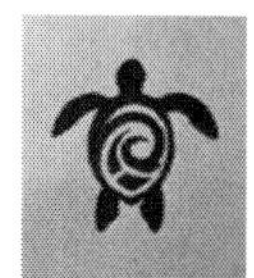

Alaka'i Lesson - Looking at Time

My upbringing combined the Protestant work ethics of my Dutch ancestors with the artistic expressions of both my parents in their careers as an interior designer and musician. This created a new concept of time. We also had a faith foundation in Christianity but were influenced by the spiritual practices of other cultures in Hawai'i. As a result I developed a dual perspective of chronos and kairos, as doing and being.

There was never a lot of pressure from my parents to succeed; however, I always did well in school. Looking back, I think there was just an inherent expectation instilled that whatever the job or responsibility, you just did your best to get the job done. And, I am the oldest of four, so responsibility came with the birth position.

Later in my teen years there was more involvement in organized activities, such as clubs and student government in school. It was in my junior year that I got my first real job at McDonalds. I quickly assimilated to the organizational structure and became a shift leader within three months which was definitely part of my *doing* more than being.

The next formal employment was as a preschool teacher, which by nature of the profession is much more about *being* and inspired me to create some personal goals toward teaching while supporting the doing dimension needed to achieve those goals. With the culture being more feminine and nurturing I was able to cultivate some significant relationships that are still a part of my support system.

One of the largest organizations I worked for was the Catholic Church. While the macro-culture of the church encompassed some shared beliefs and values, over the fifteen years of involvement, and in retrospect, it became evident there were significant disparities in the cultural differences supported by the church, particularly where I worked and worshiped. Also there was an imposed unequal power balance implied by the hierarchy and eventually my tolerance for these conflicting perspectives led to a separation.

From there I returned to the field of teaching, this time with adults. It was a very loosely defined organization where I was able to create my own structure with guidance from those in charge. It was very egalitarian and participative and began to bring me back to a *being* perspective as I was able to share that with others.

My next move landed me back into a very "doing" focused environment in retail management where everything is based on performance, including your job continuity. The being perspective is almost an afterthought. However, I was fortunate to have a manager who shared my values and beliefs and who became both mentor and friend. It was here that I felt my leadership skills both challenged and fulfilled. I started out as a part-time sales employee, but my manager also knew that I had returned to college full-time and began to allow me to take on a leadership role as well as recruit me into the management internship program for college students (albeit I was a very non-traditional student). In line with my college degree program, I was now helping with staff training and development as well as human resources.

My manager, AP*, managed with ALOHA in its fullest capacity, and at the time I wasn't even aware of those lessons. He and I connected on much more than just a business mindset, particularly when it came to the prescribed employee training that we were sent from our corporate offices. We knew that for those training messages to be received and implemented they needed to have a more culturally relevant delivery, so we would take them apart and put them back together over long coffee breaks. Over time we also connected on a more personal and spiritual level and those conversations could go on for hours. His ALOHA lessons have remained with me and continue to be a guiding star.

At the same time, being a full-time college student, I was fortunate to find myself in a department that supported both my doing and being, in that I was able to achieve both professional and personal goals. I had advisors and faculty that saw my age and experience as a benefit and skillset which eventually led to a scholarship recommendation for my Master's degree. In searching through my own journals I found a note from the professor who planted the seed of me writing a book as I entered the last semester of my master's program and the year we believed Jacob was in remission. Then as a final project, my department cohort decided that we would host an open house event for students to come and explore the opportunities offered by acquiring a Communications degree. They would be able to meet with leaders from the community who were alumni with that degree and I was selected to be the lead on organizing the event called Opening Our Doors. With her comments afterwards, my professor gave me the courage and confidence to go even further in reaching for my goals.

Following my graduation that spring, I launched Alaka'i Associates with its first logo of the turtle and the butterfly. The turtle represented wisdom, perseverance, and persistence. The wisdom of all of my Alaka'i council (mentors). The butterfly represented transformation and freedom to live the life I chose. A dotted path from the turtle to the butterfly was the first part of the journey, and waves from the butterfly to the turtle were what would carry my dreams wherever I wished to take them.

And the mission hasn't altered much since then—to teach, inspire and lead people to have a life with more meaning in the being.

Navigating Change

In my search to find balance between the doing and the being, I always had a planner and lists. One of the biggest challenges in finding balance was in my professional work and meeting all the job responsibilities and deadlines.

I came across a book that helped shift my perspective on how I approached "work." First of all I liked the title, "Getting Things Done" (David Allen, 2001) because behind the "things" I inserted "shit" in some cases. Here's part of what he subscribes to, "I consider "work," in its most universal sense, as meaning anything that you want or need to be different than it currently is. Many people make a distinction between "work" and "personal life," but I don't: to me, weeding the garden or updating my will is just as much "work" as writing a book or coaching a client." Allen also talks about how, even in 2001, the boundaries of the work world were shifting from an industrialized environment to what was termed knowledge work and dealt more directly with individuals. His approach helped me become more sensitive and adaptable to the ever-changing environment and find more balance in my "work," in all aspects of my life, personal and professional.

During this time of change I had a position that included managing communications for the nonprofit and encountered a situation where there were distinct cultural differences in the view of building professional business relationships. In a reorganization of the nonprofit they had decided that our communications in Hawaiʻi would be managed by staff in the continental U.S. It didn't take long for us to see that this was not going to work. One of the first questions I was asked from our continental counterparts, "Should we start every communication with "aloha" and end with "mahalo"? unaware that this would be highly offensive. That immediately told me that there was a lot of cultural training that needed to take place. In our island culture, it would be very disrespectful to use those terms in such a generic manner and immediately close the door to any beneficial relationship. My director in Hawaii and I responded by scheduling a cultural sensitivity training, which I designed. One of the resources I reached out to was a friend who is Hawaiian and does this kind of work for the tourist industry. He led me to an ʻōlelo noʻeau, a Hawaiian proverb, that was most appropriate to share in the perspective of navigating our own journeys.

ʻIke i ke au nui,

me ke au iki.

Know the big currents, know the little currents.

As with other sea-faring cultures, Hawaiians used nature to guide them on their journeys across the Pacific. At sea, the sun, moon, stars, wind, waves, and birds were used to navigate the canoe to its destination. A vigilant study of all these sources was paramount to a successful voyage: the destination reached and lives saved.

This ʻōlelo noʻeau, Hawaiian proverb, applied today, in terms of navigating partnerships and new ventures, reminds us that in any journey we cannot let either the big or little things go unnoticed or unanswered. What may be little to us, may be big to another. Even the smallest wave moving under the waʻa, or canoe, has something important to tell the navigator. For example, like a small wave, a simple word, misplaced or misunderstood, can upset the canoe or the relationship. Or if there is a crack in the canoe that goes unnoticed or unattended, over time even the smallest movement of the ocean can cause the canoe to break or sink, and so it is with our relationships.

And then, in Allen's book he quotes Edward Gibbons as saying, "The winds and the waves are always on the side of the navigators." And I would add, if we are paying attention, listening, watching, and adjusting our sails.

With these lessons I was able to shift my perspective and found new ways to navigate the change and keep my canoe, my balance, in both the doing and being.

Balance in the Doing and Being

During this time I was introduced to the Lōkahi Wheel through an amazing exercise. The group in the training was asked to form a circle and we were each given a 5 foot string, all attached to a ring in the middle. We were told to hold our string taut so that a raw egg could stay balanced on the ring. The egg represented our fragile life, the strings were each of the areas of your life that need to stay in balance - spirituality/soul, friends/family, work/school, feelings/emotions, and physical/body.

Then as we stood there one person was instructed to drop their string while the rest were still keeping the egg balanced. Then, two, then three strings were dropped. As you can probably imagine, at some point the egg dropped and broke.

Have you ever felt like your life was broken?

While there is no direct translation between lōkahi and balance, the two concepts can be connected when we are talking about our well-being. According to most Hawaiian dictionaries, the meaning of lōkahi is to be in one accord or agreement. So, when we are trying desperately to bring our lives into balance we use the lōkahi wheel as a tool.

Take a moment to reflect on each of the six areas and whether you feel balanced in that area and in its connection to the others. If one area is out of balance it impacts the others. For example, how does your work impact each area of the wheel and the other activities or priorities in your life? By being more mindful of the areas defined in the lōkahi wheel - you may find more balance in your life to keep your fragile “egg” intact.

Through all of these experiences, I have gained the knowledge, skills, and wisdom that I have been able to apply to all my subsequent endeavors. Being able to understand other cultural perspectives has often been the key to being able to accommodate others needs and sustain healthy relationships.

Life Changes

"And the day came when the risk to remain tight in the bud was more painful than the risk it took to blossom."
~Anais Nin

Often in the midst of your transformation you aren't even aware of what is taking place, and it isn't until you are on the other side of it that you can truly see the benefits. The butterfly has long been seen as a symbol for transformation and seems mystical and magical. But if you really study the process of that change you will find that it resembles much of how we as humans experience major life changes.

Once the caterpillar has spun its cocoon, it dissolves into a liquid substance that contains all the cells for a magnificent change, but there are very defined stages that it must go through to emerge in its fullest function as a butterfly. As humans we too have stages or phases that we go through when faced with life changes. Some may be more profound than others, and how we deal with the change can depend on which phase we are experiencing. Change often feels unexpected. More often than not we fail to recognize the stages. Like the caterpillar, the first stage is often one of falling apart. For some this can mean the dissolving of their identity and trying to hold on to the person they thought they were or waiting to "get back to normal."

The next stage in the caterpillar's metamorphosis, in that liquid substance, are these *imago* cells that contain all the instructions for the creation of the butterfly. The word imago is the root word for imagine. For us, this is the stage where we can begin to see what the life ahead of us might look like. We begin to reorganize our thinking for new possibilities.

Next, we enter the stage of reforming. This is where you stop dreaming and start implementing. Your vision starts to take shape and become more substantive. You feel a new sense of motivation. Sometimes, this stage needs repeating as you continue to re-form and refine your new life. So, expect there to be some failures and be willing to start over. Persist and persevere. Now, finally, we are reaching the last stage. As you leave the stage of reforming you are like the butterfly just emerging from the cocoon. Don't rush that stage, as like the butterfly, you must let your newly formed soggy wings have a chance to dry and strengthen before you are ready to fly.

Unexpected change can take you from calm to chaos in an instant. Having an understanding of change and the ability to navigate through it became critically important in the next stage of my life's journey.

"...gratefully and expectantly ask for one day's portion of grace..." ~ Unknown

Alaka'i Lesson - Transformation strategies

THE TRANSFORMATION STATUS REPORT 2003

What do you do when they tell you your child has a brain tumor?

It happens before you can even prepare yourself. One week your nineteen-year-old son starts having headaches, the next he starts having dizzy spells, and then begins to lose his appetite and his balance. All the clinic tells you is that it isn't an ear or sinus infection but after three weeks of progressive symptoms they recommend a CT (Computerized Axial Tomography) scan. Two days later you come out of your communication class, check your phone messages and your husband is saying, "they found something, they are admitting him, and you better get here."

You are now entering a foreign country where the language and culture overwhelm you. There are MRI'S , IV's, steroids, blood tests, pain medication, hospital gowns, and hospital beds, nurses, aides, patient services, counselors, coordinators, security, parking passes, visiting hours, cafeteria hours, sleeping in chairs, room numbers, phone numbers, and more.

The neurosurgeon tells you that he is not certain the nature of the growth but it is the size of a tennis ball and must be removed as soon as possible. He tells you that there will be several more tests to prepare for brain surgery the following week.

I step out of the room to make a series of phone calls to family and friends to tell them of the situation and ask for their prayers. I don't know what else I am supposed to do. I feel helpless and afraid, but I don't want my son to see or hear my fear. At home, I email everyone I know with the same message and the messages start coming back with offers of prayer chains, vigils, novenas, support and comfort.

After six hours of surgery and two more days for diagnosis the doctor tells you that it was a malignant tumor called medulloblastoma and will require a treatment protocol of radiation. The neurosurgeon hands you a book, The Primer of Brain Tumors (ABTA, 1998) which is the beginning of your education on brain tumors and treatment protocol. Now, comes the research because you really don't know what questions to be asking. Having access to the internet and the ability to find answers or find the right questions to ask is a tremendous support.

A medulloblastoma is a primitive neuroectodermal tumor found in the cerebellum. It is a fast-growing tumor and can spread throughout the brain and spine via the cerebrospinal fluid. This tumor is most common among children, ages three to eight, with boys twice as likely to have it than girls. Although most of these tumors occur in young children about thirty percent occur in adults. The first step to treatment is a surgical removal of as much of the tumor as possible. An MRI or CT scan of the brain is taken following surgery to determine the extent of any tumor remaining. A lumbar puncture (spinal tap) is also performed to determine if tumor cells are present in the spinal fluid. Surgery alone is not adequate treatment and is followed by radiation and/or chemotherapy. Radiation therapy usually begins within two-three weeks of surgery and conventional doses for this tumor are 5400-5600 CGY (centiGray a measurement of radiation). (ABTA, 1998)

One week after surgery our son gets to come home, just in time for Christmas. It didn't matter if anyone had gifts under the tree; we had the gift of family and friends.

Two weeks after surgery you now enter a sub-culture of the medical world known as radiation therapy. This even takes you to another "city" in that you have to travel to another hospital for the treatments on a daily basis, Monday through Friday. First you meet with the radiation oncologist who describes for you the protocol. Your son is weighed and measured and fitted with a mesh mask that will hold his head completely still while they deliver intense doses of radiation to his head and spine. The treatments themselves are painless but there are extreme side effects. Most common are fatigue, hair loss, skin changes, and nausea. Your son gets them all.

The first week into treatments Jacob is experiencing nausea and fatigue. It is so emotionally painful to watch your child endure these terrible side effects. Week after week the effects increase until he has lost so much weight that he can hardly stay hydrated and we have to put in a nutritional IV line.

Now you are taking a crash course in nursing and learning how to administer nutrition through a TPN (total parenteral nutrition) IV line. For two hours you practice under the guidance of a nurse on how to administer the medication into the nutrition bag, attach the bag to the IV line, how to operate the mechanical pump, and how to take it apart. This procedure has to be done every night and each week you have to go back in to check the IV and pick up more nutrition bags. This goes on for two and a half weeks.

Once radiation ends, we move to a different "city" called physical therapy. One of the side effects of the tumor's location in relation to the brain and from surgery is that your son's physical capabilities are affected. The left side of his body does not have the muscular strength or coordination that it had prior to the tumor so once a week he goes to therapy to retrain and regain those physical capacities. It is hard work and frustrating. This 19 year old wants to be his "old self" and it will take time, patience, and hard work to get there.

At three and six months after surgery there are follow-up MRI's and blood tests, which show promising results. There is no change evident around the surgical site and white blood cell counts are almost normal. The doctor says that the next six months should show weight gain and strength returning. You now look forward to the next visit in anticipation of good news but always carrying in the back of your mind a little "what if?"

I have nursed this son through a car accident at five years old, which left him in a body cast for three months and now this. So, what do you do when they tell you your son has a brain tumor? What was I supposed to learn? That life is precious, prayer has power, and to take life one day at a time.

Addendum:: The "what if" came in 2004 when the tumor returned. Again surgery, this time chemotherapy, and a year later it metastasized to his bone. The hardest part of being a caregiver came as we journeyed with Jacob to his crossing at home, with the support of a wonderful palliative care team, and were surrounded by family and very close friends.

Under a Full Moon and Guiding Star

The night of December 14, 2005, was crisp and clear, with a full moon and stars casting their light down on us while we sat with Jacob as he took his last breath. I recall stepping outside into that light afterwards and looking up and locking that heavenly light and energy into my heart. In the Hawaiian moon calendar there are 30 phases, one of which is Māhealani, and that was where it was that night. And so every year in that December moon phase I can see his face smiling. A few months after his transition, two of our dearest friends gifted us with a star registered in Jacob's name with the International Star Registry where they had found that on that particular night the constellation over us was Aries (Jacob's and my astrological sign) and so the star assigned to him was in that constellation. It is an incredible gift to know that in the years that have followed, in December, I can know that his light is shining brightly overhead.

In The Garden

I come to the garden alone,
While the dew is still on the roses,
And the voice I hear, falling on my ear,
The Son of God discloses.
And He walks with me, and He talks with me,
And He tells me I am His own,
And the joy we share as we tarry there,
None other has ever known.

~ C. Austin Miles

A Father's Journey

Many times, I have shared with friends and family that Jacob's transition was the most difficult time in my life and yet also the most enlightening. The one experience most meaningful came a few days before Jacob returned home to our Creator. He was in palliative care at the time so we were all home with him. I was deep in thought, wondering why this was happening, and praying that Jacob was at peace. I had several "real" questions for God. It was at this time that I felt a strong pain in my chest and it seemed to be gaining strength. It didn't occur to me to consider medical care, instead my solution was to enter this darkness in my chest as deeply as I could. I laid in our bed and focused all my attention on it. As I laid there the pain began to subside and I came to an understanding that was delivered without words. I became aware that Our Creator's love was eternal and peace was my only outcome. We didn't need anyone's approval, be it an individual or institution. We are one with God. There can be no path for us other than God's eternal Love. As difficult as the time was, I now know that Jacob was safe and at peace in the heart of God. Love has no opposite. ~ Joaquin

Blank Pages

What do they say to you? As I proceeded with my writing endeavors I was often facing the blank pages which are sometimes inviting and other times frustrating. In the months after Jacob's transition, I came across a journal that he had started years before which had been left on the shelf. The first few pages had wonderful photos, articles, quotes, but it was cut short, as was his life. Some of the inspiration in those first pages was truly a reflection of where he was in his life. A photo of a street sign with an arrow that said, "My Way", a list of ideas for creating a quieter world, a dinner blessing that was his grandfather's favorite, thoughts on forgiveness, and more. Here is one I especially like:

"Even when I'm feeling low, I can always find solace in nature, a restorative when dealing with pain. Wonder heals through an alchemy of the mind." ~ Author unknown

At first I didn't want to intrude on his "space" but now its blank pages invited me to continue his story. The story of the life he has inspired in me. Those blank pages hold endless possibilities to fill.

"Within your heart, keep one still, secret spot where dreams may go." ~ Louise Driscoll

PART II: BEING AND BECOMING

Partners in the Mystery

"Human beings have been trying to solve problems at the "doingness" level for a long time, without much success. That's because true change is always made at the level of "being," not "doing." ~ Conversations with God, Bk.3, Neale Donald Walsch

---

Presently, I begin each day with a meditation practice outside. Being in touch with nature is my "church". In the quiet of the morning, sometimes with a cup of hot tea, I will listen to a guided meditation and then spend some time writing my own reflection to set the tone for my day. Along with my meditation and journaling, I make a post that always has the hashtag "livealohalivewell" to remind myself and others that you need to live the values of ALOHA together in order to live well. But it's taken years to develop it as a foundational habit. While it would be ideal to build that foundation early in life, often it comes with years of experience and wisdom gained along the way.

When I was born I was baptized into the Methodist church where my parents were members. I attended church and Sunday school up until I was confirmed as a teenager. And in those teenage years my parents' lives began to shift away from being active in the church, and so did mine. But that opened up new experiences in those years.

One of those teenage summers the word got around that there was an itinerant preacher in town with a Pentecostal church who was young and very attractive. Being a typical teenage follower I went with the crowd to see for myself. There was lots of excitement in "belonging" so there were many conversions and baptisms, but that all waned once he left. What I was left with was not any particular attachment to the religion but a desire to belong to a faith community and a new experience of my spirituality that was a stepping stone for more growth.

My next step on my path of spirituality came when I got married. I was introduced to my husband's religious upbringing as a Catholic and because it was something so central to his identity at the time, we committed to raising our family within that faith community. We became very involved as lay ministers and

Sunday School teachers, and even became paid staff of the parish. But the source of our spirituality was still untapped.

I recall an experience in my early thirties that placed firmly in my consciousness that we are not merely human beings trying to have a spiritual experience but really the other way around. That our spirits and essence go far beyond that physical existence. It was the last time I saw my grandpa. Traveling with my father back to the small rural town of Lewellen, Nebraska, we had been preoccupied with funeral arrangements the moment we arrived. The reality of Grandpa Jake's death had not really hit me yet. Then the moment arrived as the family queued up inside this little church to pay our last respects. I hear my twin aunts in front of me commenting, "He looks like he's asleep in his easy chair." "Doesn't he look natural."

As I approach the casket I am surprised at my own reaction. I say to myself, but really in response to my aunts, "He doesn't look 'natural' at all. That's not my grandfather lying there." My Grandpa Jake was a tall, sturdy man with a vibrant spirit and that body there was not him! I feel confused and so I walk back alone, down the lane behind the church that leads to my grandparents house. As I arrive at the back yard gate, I am welcomed by the rows of gladioli and roses, of carrots, corn, and string beans in the garden my grandfather tended with love. He would come home at lunch to water and again after work in it in the evening shade. It's as if he is standing there. I can feel his presence. I can almost see him, with his pants rolled up, bending over to pull a weed. My confusion dissipates. The vision fades, but I know for certain that he is still with me.

My next encounter with my emerging spirituality came with a course I took as I continued to chip away at my bachelor's degree requirements between work and family life. It was a course on world religions and at the time I was working for the Catholic church. I began to question and challenge the perspective of women in religion and here's what emerged.

In that course I became keenly aware of the confines of religion, particularly that of the Catholic church, and its patriarchal structure that caused me to struggle as I was learning and yearning to grow in my own identity. I was discovering that I longed for the acknowledgment and affirmation that I am from Source, a part of the Divine. That I have all the elements of that Divine duality to be of service within or outside of any particular religious construct. I had started to uncover my spiritual consciousness in the idea that we are all spiritual beings having a human experience and not humans seeking to have a spiritual experience. I also gained an understanding that this concept of spirituality is ancient and vast as well as shared across time.

Here is an excerpt from a paper I wrote, Partners in the Mystery.

In all ages and in all places, men have conceived of a Great Mother. These Great Mothers, whose worship has dominated the religious thoughts of peoples far removed from each other in time, space, and culture, have an essential similarity which cannot be anything less than amazing. Women's role in religion is rooted in primitive, animalistic aspects and yet each generation seems to struggle with this role. In the 1980's this struggle or search for identity was labeled feminist theology. In this, there are three archetypes that can be personified as feminine: the mother, the maid, and the anima. The great mother archetype has a dual nature, both good and bad. She is connected with both birth and death, and represents the duality in both men and women. From the point of view of Judeo-Christianity tradition, the soul has always been represented with a feminine nature. Its mysteries, its flights, its bid for attention, have been likened to the nature of a woman. As a result, the woman is endowed with the burden of being a link or intercessor to another world. Two female figures that come close to that God/Source membership are recognized as Sophia—the personification of Wisdom, or as Mary—the compassionate Mother of God. The feminine dimension of the Divine was repressed for many years by religious constructs, but has slowly returned to our spiritual consciousness. All women have a special ministry, not only those in religious confines. We must return to our connection to the Great Mothers that have guided us for generations.

The response to my paper from a Catholic nun who was my boss, and who I perceived as a mentor at the time, was less than enthusiastic. I sensed that she found it confrontational towards her place and position within the structure and community she had chosen. But my world had opened up.

Then, everything about my spirituality changed when we went through our experience with our son, Jacob's, cancer journey. Our family discovered the profound difference between religion and spirituality, the second being unbound by walls and rules and judgment. Spirituality embraces only love. The true lessons of ALOHA began to be revealed from here on for all generations of our family to come.

My son, Joshua, who is four years older than Jacob and a chaplain reminds us of this legacy here which he calls, Raising Caregivers.

During the annual and traditionally Mexican Día de los Muertos, my family creates a ritual display called an ofrenda (offering)—a home altar—for loved ones who have died like my younger brother Jacob. This spiritual act of remembrance brings continued healing, opens the way for heart-talk, and renews the minds of the faithful. An especially meaningful time for young and old caregivers alike, it came as no surprise that my daughter Maria, springing from her own spiritual reflection after coworking with her brother Jacob to decorate our altar, asked me with all the innocence and wonder of a child: "What were Uncle Jake's last words?"

Now I have found parenting to be a continuance of the journey for caregivers—be it mākua (parent), kupuna (grandparent), ʻanakala (uncle), ʻanakē (auntie), kaikuaʻana (older brother or sister), or whomever the ʻohana (family) may be. As ancestor and descendant, the caregiver stands in a place where one can trust their sense of belonging and connection (receiving the care they need), where one feels the pulse of all that ever was, is now, and ever will be (the primal blessing of life). For this reason, we acknowledge that in receiving care – in being given that costly grace, we are given the opportunity to raise caregivers who will not only extend that grace, but who will multiply it for generations.

The journey of a caregiver starts at their upbringing—the raising of a caregiver: the gentle yet strong care necessitated by their infancy—the great love that loved them first; then it's the direction they receive as a child—faintly glimpsing a long obedience in the same direction; followed by the guidance accepted (or not) as an adolescent and young adult—the healthy realization that the set of footprints in the sand may not be their own; and culminating in the steadfast support offered to the new adult from the old(er) adult—a humbling reminder that we don't have to have the last words…those have already been sealed on our hearts with aloha. May you be blessed.

Connections

"We must be willing to get rid of the life we planned, so as to have the life that is waiting for us." ~ Joseph Campbell

---

Our family's journey of spirituality also led to new experiences with the native intelligence and cultures which brought together Native American, Native Hawaiian and our connection to the green sea turtle or *honu* as our *'aumakua* (protector/animal spirit). That connection began when three educational trainers came to the school where Jacob attended. One of the first lessons they taught was in protecting the honu, which was, and still is, on the Endangered Species list. Those trainers also became my mentors and that relationship spanned more than 30 years.

In the busy *"doing"* years I was privileged to meet some very special individuals, CT* and MR*. CT* was a ray of sunlight! She had long blonde hair, and coupled with her bright spirit and smile, she simply radiated positivity. MR* was a gentle spirit raised in the 60's and always willing to turn a teaching moment into a learning one.

They were contracted to provide consulting for our educational team—administrators, faculty, and staff—on a particular model of teaching and coaching at the parochial parish and school where I worked and our children attended on the island of Oahu. In that training they used my son Jacob's fourth grade class as a model classroom with the themed topic of the humpback whale which migrates to Hawaii every year to give birth and mate. They asked the children to draw a humpback whale from a picture they showed and were amazed at Jacob's talent, at age ten, to draw his picture almost to scale. They immediately asked me if they could continue to mentor him in another program they had created on the island of Maui providing environmental education to kids and families. Now, here are two relative strangers asking to take my ten year old to another island. While I was immediately excited, it took a bit of convincing for my husband to agree. That summer was the first of many. And while Jacob did the first one solo, after that I accompanied him. While they began mentoring him I was gaining additional mentoring as well.

CT* in particular was one of the most positive and uplifting individuals I have ever encountered, and you couldn't help but be impacted by her energy. She is the one who introduced me to the power of praise, and how it is the foundation of building trust in relationships. You "catch" someone doing good, encourage the right behavior, and without criticizing any errors guide and coach them in the right direction. Praise in the truest and most honest form is what makes a lasting impression and is most valued by those that receive it.

There are also some specific techniques for giving that kind of meaningful praise. First, it must be immediate. Second, it must be specific. Tell the person how their actions or efforts had or will have a positive effect on others or the organization where it took place. And, finally, encourage them to do more. Help people reach their full potential by catching them doing something right. Honest praise also sends some critical life messages, such as: I believe in you, I trust you, I know you can do it, you are listened to, you are cared for, and you are very important.

However, there are also some cautions when giving praise. Liken it to growing a flower: don't over fertilize or over water, and sometimes praise needs to be pruned because if you get too verbose with it, it loses its impact; and be sure you have the right gardening tools for the job (i.e. post-it notes, thank you cards, and handwritten letters still have the best effects). I have kept many of the "praise notes" she sent me and they continue to remind me to keep that positive focus in all my endeavors.

CT*, and her partner MR*, soon had an impact on our whole family, coaching our daughter with her educational goals, as well as supporting us through Jacob's transition. As part of our journey with CT* and MR*, both Jacob and I wrote research papers on the fibropapilloma tumors that were being found on the honu. One of the primary researchers in that field was a man named George Balaz, whom we later came to know personally in an ironic twist of fate in regards to tumors.

In the year after his first bout with brain cancer, surgery and radiation, all Jacob wanted to do was to be able to go back to Maui to snorkel to see the honu and go on a humpback whale watch. We made it happen. On the day of the whale watch, as we are coming back into the harbor, one of his mentors, MR*, invites him to narrate for the other guests on the boat about the honu that we are seeing. Reluctantly, Jacob begins his "scientific" talk about the honu and as he goes to point out a pair next to the boat realizes that they are coupling,mating, and isn't quite sure what to say, so he says, "You can see these two swimming together." Well, MR*, says, "Oh no, they are mating!"

and Jacob blushes. About a year later, as Jacob was at the end of his earthly journey and in the hospital, this story got relayed to that well-known honu researcher, George Balaz, through his wife who was a social worker at the hospital. A few days later, she came back with a large print of a photo, as a gift from her husband, of two honu "swimming together". That photo is framed and hangs in our home, always providing for a good story with guests. The presence of a honu is now a sign for all of our family that Jacob's presence is near.

One of our last big moments with CT* and MR* was when we spread part of Jacob's ashes off the coast of Lahaina, Maui. We had spent a lot of time in those waters on humpback whale (koholā) watches and swimming with the honu (green sea turtles). On the day we went out, they had arranged a boat for us, but CT* had gone on ahead earlier in a pontoon boat to find a location for us out in the middle, the piko/navel, of the ocean between Maui, Lāna'i, and Kaho'olawe. It was a remarkably perfect day; clear blue skies and the most clear calm waters I have ever seen, reflecting that blue sky. The particular spot was a divine choice as there were two koholā resting there. As if on cue, as our boat approached they began to move in the most gentle ballet. Swimming near us with slow quiet elegance, raising their backs and tails out of the water. Once the captain stopped the engine, they continued for a few minutes and then moved a distance away but still within view.

We began our ceremony with a Hawaiian oli or chant, E Hōmai, which is often used to open a special occasion and calls on our ancestors to be with us at that moment. Then as we scattered his ashes we could see them spiraling down through the clear water with the sun reflecting on them, looking like glitter or small diamonds. Several of us slowly lowered ourselves into the water to fully connect with the moment, and it was as though that message had reached those two koholā because they started to move back towards us. Then in a final farewell, they turned in the direction of O'ahu and simultaneously did a fluke (tail) up dive, a sign to us from Jacob as he always gave a double "shaka" sign. A hui hou, until we meet again. CT* and MR* have now joined Jacob and together continue to guide us in living ALOHA.

Fifteen years after Jacob's transition, our daughter, Paloma, who is an elementary school principal, was invited to join an educational group focused on the teachings of ALOHA by Aunty Pilahi Paki*, through Pono Shim. In an extension of that, she was also invited to a group called LiveAloha. In her very first meeting, on Zoom, another participant introduces himself with the last name Balaz. She followed up and, as our family has come to know how the Universe (and Jacob) operate, it was George's son. Again, spirituality embraces only love—ALOHA—and connects us, generation after generation. (*ALOHA)

The Path to Wellness

"Like a wildflower, she spent her days allowing herself to grow, not many knew of her struggle, but eventually all knew of her light." ~ *Nikki Rowe*

All of that spiritual growth has also led me to focus on my personal health and wellness. As I look back on my journey as an adult, and my opportunities to care for others, I have always had a basic understanding of what it meant to be healthy—eat fresh foods, exercise, get enough sleep—but in the midst of that crazy "doing" life of caregiver, with a husband and four kids, health and self care often took a back seat. And over time, that stress compounded into health problems like migraines and IBS (irritable bowel syndrome) which would sometimes have me in the emergency room. I would have times where I would bring wellness back into focus, but at one point, in a toxic work environment, I became keenly aware that my health had to come first. I had to repair and refill my cup before I had any more to share with others. This is where I learned the value of daily habits of self care and stress management and began to implement them in my life.

That personal development led me to envision having my own wellness business where I could share those lessons with others and that is where Alaka'i Associates was reborn, with a mission to help others lead activated lives in abundance, to bring health and wellness and wealth to my family and the world. I want to continue to deepen my awareness of my spirituality and connect it with all that I endeavor. I want to share that connection with others with love and acceptance. And, I want to give thanks for the abundance it brings to my life.

Learning to Pause and Breathe

I vividly remember that pivotal moment in learning the power of a pause and breath. As humans we are hardwired to survive and when our life seems threatened fear can cause us to hold our breath, but at some point we must come up for air, sometimes gasping for it. That moment happened when Jacob was hit by the car in front of our house. By the time I was out the front door it had already happened, and as I rushed to my child laying in the street a neighbor gently stepped in front of me, held my shoulders and said, "breathe." I don't recall a physical response to this moment but I do know that hearing that word from someone else triggered a calming effect for me to be more present in that moment. In the 30-plus years since then there have been many more times when crisis or fear has taken my breath away. I began to see how even in our daily lives the stressors cause us to hold our breath. Unknowingly, when we tense up, and are not breathing fully or deeply, we are depriving our bodies of the oxygen it needs to function at its full capacity. Over the years, learning breathing techniques has led me to an awareness of this critical function, and I have incorporated those techniques into my daily habits.

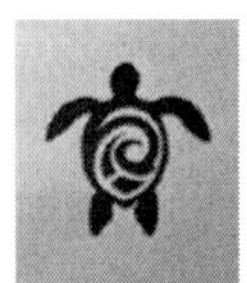

Alaka'i Lesson - Breathe

Conversations with the Universe

"There are years that ask questions and years that answer." ~ Zora Neale Hurston

"Live the questions now…" ~ Rainier Maria Rilke

In my transformation from the doing to being, and the spiritual awakening that also took place along the way, I found myself changing my previously perceived image of God from a male voice to one that encompassed something much greater. As humans we seem to want to label that energy and presence with a pronoun that is so limiting, but I began to see it as something that was much more vast and powerful, that embodied all - Creator, Source, Universe.

In my human capacity I had lots of "why" questions about the events of my life. You know the "why me?" or the "why did _____ happen?" The questions that were focused inward. But over time, and through that greater lens, my questions became more focused outward towards who, what, when, where, and how. And those are the questions that Creator, Source, and the Universe love to hear. If you are open and accepting of the answers they will come, not always in the way you expected, but they will come. Sometimes the answers may take years, but be ready, because when they come they can be fast and more than you expected.

So, if you find that there is a small ember that keeps burning inside you, that creative spark that keeps occurring over and over throughout your life - know that it is the Universe telling you that you are not done yet. That spark is what you came into the world with, and only you can fan the flame.

 Alaka'i Lesson - Golden Ember and Be A Tree

My kukui tree helps me remember my spark, my light. The kukui is also known as the candlenut tree. It is considered one of the "canoe plants" that arrived with Polynesian migration, with many uses including medicinal, food, dye and waterproofing for kapa, and fishing, but most revered for its role as both a literal and spiritual source of light. In recent tradition, it has come to symbolize enlightenment, knowledge, protection, guidance, peace, and learning.

This Hawaiian proverb or 'ōlelo no'eau is said to have been originally cited by a Tahitian mother to her son, which poetically links the continuation of the 'ohana (family) and their enlightenment with the illumination shed by a chain of kukui seeds. "The seed was sown. It budded, it blossomed. It spread out and budded again and joined line on line, like the candlenut strung on one stem. 'Tis lighted. It burns aglow and sheds its light o'er the land.

In my journey from doing to being, I heard about a book called *Simple Abundance*, by Sarah Ban Breathnach (1995). With that book in hand, I began a year long exploration and excavation into discovering myself. A year of self care. A year of reflection and change.

One of the first lessons was to begin a gratitude journal. When put into daily practice, gratitude has a profound impact on how you see the world and how the world responds to you. Just starting with three things you are grateful for each day, either morning or evening, is really fundamental to self care and a habit that you can build on. And that is what I did. Journaling had been something I did off and on as an adult, but here is where it became my voice and my vision.

Journaling has many forms and formats and one that I especially love is an activity from *Simple Abundance* called the Discovery Journal. Using a blank artist's sketchbook, you cut out and paste in pictures of anything that brings you joy or inspiration—people, places, things—to help uncover your authentic self. For example, I love photos of women in just blue jeans and a white shirt. Yes, that's me, although I have foregone the white shirt because they are an invitation for a stain of some sort. But that is my preferred style: simple comfort. It is quite revealing to keep creating these journals as you can see yourself evolve over time. Other journals are those that chronologically track my journey as a woman and the many roles and roads I have traversed. My lessons with journaling and daily habits will continue to unfold as time goes on.

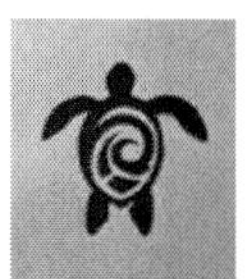
Alaka'i Lesson - Discovery Journal

Being and Becoming Alaka'i

The first emergence of Alaka'i Associates was intended to be a personal and professional development consulting business, providing training for individuals and small businesses with team building and collaboration skills. Its name was chosen by my dear friend and mentor, AP*, whose knowledge of Hawaiian culture prompted the use of the word, alaka'i, which means leader or guide. It is the value of leadership to lead with initiative, with integrity, and with your good example. I was very honored, and even when I had to close that business down for a time, I never gave up on the name. The original logo represented my journey of persistence with a honu and transformation with a butterfly. I carry both those images with me as tattoos.

The new Alaka'i Associates emerged when I turned 60 years old. That's a significant milestone so I took a week's vacation that began with a women's retreat. Part of my personal growth that weekend was that I could see how Alaka'i would return as a wellness business. Since I was still working full time with the American Cancer Society, and that retirement number of 65 was a ways off, I started with redesigning my logo, website, and starting a blog. That commitment kept me going and writing.

But something else profound happened that week. With my new commitment to Alaka'i I began cleaning and reorganizing the room in my home that would be my office, my creative space. In the back of the closet I found this large envelope and what I pulled out was the MRI film of Jacob's first tumor, the size of a tennis ball. ***I LOST IT!!*** I was mad! I was cussing and damning that film and cancer every which way I could. I went in search of the largest, black trash bag I could find, threw that envelope in it, tied it with a vengeance, marched out to the trash can, tossed it in and slammed it shut, saying, "Cancer doesn't define me anymore!" And then I cried. A very cathartic cry. That was when I knew that my mission and destiny was to move into a space of health and wellness and bring that to the world — one person at a time.

As I said, one of the first things I did to rebirth Alaka'i Associates was to create a new website and begin writing a blog, because, in case you hadn't quite yet noticed, I like to write! I had years of journals to pull from to start me off, and it was good training for what I saw on the horizon. My early website blogs were mostly short clips from those journals, or brief meditations and insights. They also were my way of introducing myself and my mission to the world. Here are a few of my early favorites that connect to the elements that embrace my family because of their connection to ALOHA.

April 17, 2017

Honu...you may have noticed my affinity for honu (green sea turtle). It first began with Jacob's connection to CT* and MR*, his mentors who were the ocean educators on Maui. Jacob had a gift for drawing and was mentored by them through the Ocean Project. His drawings are still seen on their rack cards all over Maui for the KIDS program.

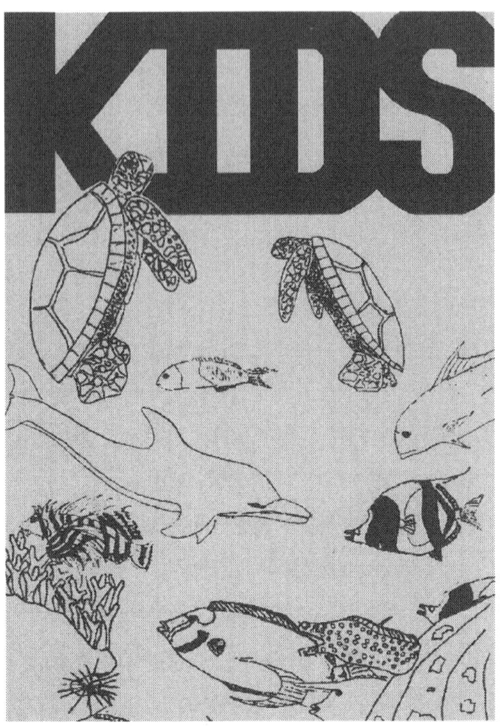

Both Jacob and I did research projects on the tumors that were being found on the honu and we became strong advocates for protection of the green sea turtle. Through Jacob's cancer journey, the honu became our family ʻaumakua (guardian spirit). The turtle is known to represent wisdom, perseverance, and persistence. Over the years, we have had many wonderful experiences with honu, letting us know that Jacob is always with us.

April 19, 2017

Another very strong spirit animal in my journey is the koholā (humpback whale). My experience with them also started with Jacob's involvement with the Ocean Project in Maui. These majestic giants grace our Hawaiian waters every year after a long journey from the northern Pacific and whale watching on Maui is one of my favorite activities and actually has sometimes been a very spiritual experience. If you ever have the opportunity to be up close to a koholā and look into their eyes you can just tell there is an ancient wisdom they possess. This became another environmental advocacy issue for us to support, and for several years we participated in the annual Humpback Whale Sanctuary Count, and I encourage you to try it, at least once.

"Life is not measured by the breaths you take, but by the moments that take your breath away." ~ Unknown

HĀ - The Breath of Life

In the month right before Jacob's transition, a very special spiritual being came into our lives. At the time my daughter was teaching at an elementary school and taking time off to help with her brother's care. Her fellow teachers had met Jacob and knew that he had been studying Hawaiian culture and played the 'ukulele, so they asked if a new teacher at the school who was teaching Hawaiian Studies and was a musician could come visit Jacob. We agreed, and soon after, one evening there was a knock at the door and there he was, Walt Keale Mix. A stocky man with long wavy hair pulled back in a ponytail and while he could have seemed imposing, came in with a quiet humility. He and Jacob started their conversation with Walt telling him about his background and his connection to a rather famous local Hawaiian musical family. Jacob stopped him abruptly at one point and said, "So, if you are Hawaiian, shouldn't we be greeting each other with a honi?" A honi is a traditional greeting shared by many Polynesian cultures where you greet each other forehead to forehead in an exchange of breath—your hā—your life force. Something spiritual happened in that moment as later, after Jacob's transition, Walt told us that he felt the presence of all our ancestors and knew that we were connected through them. After that first meeting he continued to come and would play some of the music he was writing for Jacob on his 'ukulele and share stories about their lives.

But Walt wasn't just playing music and sharing stories with Jacob, he was ministering to him as well. In one of his last visits, after Jacob had gone into a coma, he came to wash his feet and bestowed on him a very special kīhei, a garment worn by

Hawaiian leaders and kahu (religious). And as our family witnessed this we knew he was also ministering to us, touching each of us where we were on our journeys. Our relationship grew even further as Walt was also a pastor of a small unconventional church called The Gathering. While Christian-based, it brought together people who were searching for something outside the structure inside four walls. We met at the beach and shared both our human and spiritual experiences. It was a place where it was less about "doing" church and more about "being" church. Regardless of any differences, what we had was a community.

That community became part of our family as new generations were born. Our grandchildren's Hawaiian middle names were bestowed by our dear friend, Walt, who carries a long Hawaiian lineage and became close to our family as he came to minister to Jacob in his last days.

"When a Hawaiian name is bestowed, a connection is made, a story told, history preserved, someone honored, a hope expressed."

(* hawaiian-naming-traditions)

Each name carries a connection to Jacob and each child's personality fully embodies their name.

Helamakanimaikaponookaiwiahaula — the voice of the righteous ancestor speaks again (as the first grandchild this one carries the voices of the ancestors, especially Jacob, with her)

Kalāho`onani — the sun/Son rises in glory (this child is up with the sun and his father is a chaplain)

'Ehukaiaka'ena — the wind and mist dance off the waves of three special locations along the coast of Oahu (this child brings that joy of the ocean with her everywhere)

Māhealani — one of the Hawaiian moon phases that comes just after a full moon (Jacob transitioned the night of a full moon, and this child was born in this moon phase with all that full moon energy)

This was and is a true gift of ALOHA.

In my journals and Alaka'i blog further reflections on those elements followed:

The Wind....

The wind, most commonly known in Hawaiian as makani, has so many more names to describe it in all its forms from soft breezes to howling winds, from salty sea air to cool mountain air. For me, makani is the breath and voices of ancestors letting me know they are near.

Rain, mist, & mountains,

Voices in the wind

Telling me you are here.

Paying attention to the wind is a lesson in listening to not just what is outside, the physical manifestations, but to what is inside yourself, the spiritual awakenings. Take time this week to stop and listen to the wind. In Hawaiian culture the multitude of names for the wind include the where, when, and how of each different type of wind, whether it's a whispering breeze or a howling storm. In embracing ALOHA the "HĀ" refers to the wind inside of you - your breath, and in living ALOHA that HĀ must be an exchange of spirit between individuals and all of creation.

The Sun....

Kalāho`onani—loosely translated means "Here comes the beautiful sun" and in a more spiritual reference "Son". It is a constant reminder of renewal and new beginnings. It brings warmth and energy to fill each day. And sometimes it is just enough to sit and feel the sun—not think, not write, just be. I have been blessed to live in a place where the sun gives a special touch to the natural beauty that surrounds us. It brings an intensity to the colors and shapes of our environment, the brightness of the blue in sky and sea, the crisp green outline of our majestic mountains, and the rainbow of color in our flowers. Thank you, Creator, for this gift!

The Sea....

Kai is one of the Hawaiian words for the ocean which is one of the places that connects with me in special ways. Born in Hawai'i, the beach was a place where as a baby, even without my memory, it became a connecting place for me. As a young child I learned to swim holding my father's hand and diving through a crashing wave learning to respect the power of the ocean as well as enjoy its capacity for joy. As I grew older it took on a more social significance as I spent hours in the water with friends and family. Further along I began to understand my role in protecting the ocean and all that lived there. Having an opportunity to scuba dive, I found a whole new world and developed a new level of understanding. And now, most profoundly, it is the home of the honu, which has become our family's ʻaumakua (guardian spirit) and reminder of Jacob's presence. As the words of the song, by Israel Kamakawiwo'ole, *White Sandy Beach*, say, "...the sounds of the ocean soothe my restless soul."

The Moon….

Mahina and Māhealani are two Hawaiian words associated with the moon and have a special connection for me. Somehow the full moon has always had a powerful energy, so much so that I would have to be careful if I was driving on the night of a full moon because I would just be mesmerized by it. Even more so if it was rising on a clear night and reflecting off the ocean! That image became even more significant with Jacob during his cancer journey as he would visualize himself riding on the back of a giant honu under a full moon, and he crossed over on the night of a full moon. And then five years ago, Māhealani came shining into our lives again in the month of December, as Jacob's nephew came into our world. That full moon is most certainly a portal for coming in and going out of this physical realm. So, tonight or on the next full moon I invite you to stop and stand in the moonlight and feel that light and energy that connects us all.

Alaka'i Lesson - A Peaceful Place

Another lesson of ALOHA was revealed in our journey with Jacob in his last few months before he transitioned. Our long-time friends and godparents to our middle son, Joshua, have a daughter Colleen who was born just two weeks before Jacob. We often said they were twins from different wombs. Colleen's sister, Brigid, knew how much Jacob liked the musician Jack Johnson and made this incredible connection for us. During that time, Jacob ended up hospitalized and all he really wanted was to be home for his final days. During that hospital stay, Brigid contacted Jack Johnson to see if she might be able to get an autographed CD or poster for Jacob. One day, much to our surprise, as we are sitting in Jacob's hospital room, a phone call comes in. I answered the phone and Jacob motioned to me that he did not want to talk with anyone. I smiled and said, "Yes, I think you do. This is Jack Johnson!" Before he took the phone he motioned to his father and Colleen to leave the room, which we all found amusing, as that was typical of his personality. He talked for about 20 minutes and ended the call by giving Jack our home phone number. Jack's career was taking off at the time and we appreciated his ALOHA in reaching out but never expected more.

A few weeks later, at home, the phone rings, and yes, it's him, sharing his ALOHA again. It meant so much to Jacob as well as the rest of our family. But we weren't done with the connections. At the same time, Walt Keale, who was ministering to Jacob with his music, asked if he could borrow Jacob's ukulele for a few days. We said sure not really knowing why. It turns out that he was recording at Jack Johnson's studio so had him sign the ukulele. More ALOHA transforming our lives. We continue to be inspired by both Jack and Walt, not only through their music but by the way they strive to live ALOHA to its fullest meaning. Our family theme song is one of Jack's compositions, *Better Together.*

The Power of Friends

Out in the middle of the ocean, on stormy seas, that's how I felt during our journey with Jacob's cancer. Sometimes feeling like my ship was about to sink and looking for something to keep me afloat. That's where I developed the "lifeboat theory".

Most of us are familiar with what a lifeboat is and how it is used. You know, women and children first, and always one person in the boat who guides everyone else to safety. Many times, in the midst of life's storms, we rely on that one person (sometimes more) to keep us afloat.

Who is in your lifeboat? Find at least five people—the ones you can count on one hand. Those friends who, even though you may live miles or even countries apart, are still there for you when you need a lifeline at 3 a.m, when you are "knee deep in a river and dying of thirst." *(song by Kathy Matea)* Throughout my life I have become more mindful and appreciative of those life savers.

I have been fortunate to have some life-long lifelines with a handful of women, three of whom I have known for over 60 years. We met in elementary school, had birthdays and slumber parties together, and while our lives took separate paths after high school we stayed connected over the years with occasional visits and the annual Christmas card.

Somehow the bonds of friendship forged when we were young were strong enough to stand the test of time. So, as we approached our 50th birthday year we decided it was time for a reunion. We agreed to rent a beach house on the island of

Hawai'i. LL* lived there so she collected us all at the airport, but before we drove out to the beach house we had to make a stop at a well-known restaurant that has been around since our youth and share our first meal together. Food is always a great ice-breaker. After our hearty meal of both food and conversation we headed to our retreat for the weekend. In true beach-house fashion it was designed to be open to the sights, sounds, and smells of our tropical surroundings. After settling into our choice of rooms we headed out to the tide pools where we were refreshed and renewed by the cold ocean waters. The weekend proceeded with more food fresh from a farmers' market, shopping, and lots more conversation. It was like we had never been apart; it was as though we were still living down the street from each other. At first, we reminisced about our youth, with special teachers and first boyfriends. Then we caught up on our adult lives of relationships, marriages, divorces, children, and pets (who for some were very much like their children).

My favorite part of all were the comments these three left in my journal at the end of the weekend:

LL* - "This has been restorative and fun. It is so amazing to count the years. I hope we get to do this again. Adding to the long list of memories. I hope we can still remember the childhood stuff next time. It is so cool that we all remember different parts and this is good. Thanks for all the love and friendship."

JR* - "Roses are red, violets are blue, We couldn't have done this if it wasn't for you! Thanks for keeping us young. Stay cool."

LC* - "It is so good to reconnect! I've missed you! What a joy to see your folks again as well. I look forward to the new tradition of getting together as bigger kids and playing. Thank you for being a part of the corporate memory. Between all of us we seem to have one memory that is really detailed! See you next year."

That time together was so special for us we decided that in the second half of our lives we wouldn't let time keep us apart and since then there have been more adventures to the San Juan islands and Yosemite, and soon to include Scotland. Each time we connect we reforge that bond, becoming stronger both individually and collectively. I truly believe we have not only added life to our years but years to our lives.

Here is where I began to really recognize and appreciate each of these women for the elements they represent and how they bring those elements to my life. LL* was the first of the three that I met when we were seven years old. We lived next door to each other and she is the creative, independent spirit. The Air that moved in and out and around. Her passion has always been in costume designing. LC* is next. She lived just around the block and is the grounded one, loving and living with the Earth. Her passion led her to become a botanist. And third is JR* who I always felt was the stable one, the Wood, and her passion led her to become an educator and writer. And then there's me — the Fire — always ready to ignite and reignite our connections. These three women were there when my first child was born and to hold me up when my fourth child was re-diagnosed with brain cancer. They are my definition of the Lifeboat Theory. We continue to support each other across the miles and continents on our life journeys.

"Friends I can count on..." *(song by Kathy Matea)*

I recently came across a little book called *The Power of A Woman* that was given to me more than 20 years ago by another wonderful friend that talks about the capacity within each woman to touch others with love, faith, and action. It came at a perfect time in my life back then as my children were getting older, and I was beginning to find my identity beyond being a full-time mother and wife. It is a collection of wisdom from generations of women who have paved a way for those who came after them. I have cherished this little book not so much for its content but for the special message my friend wrote, in that the powers of love, faith, and action were what she admired about me. That is how I want to be remembered and so it serves as a reminder to keep those powers ever-present on my journey. Thank you, AC*.

Here are just a few of my favorite gems from the book:

Love is a fruit in season at all times, and within reach of every hand. ~ Mother Teresa

******

It is this belief in a power larger than myself and other than myself which allows me to venture into the unknown and even the unknowable... ~ Maya Angelou

******

If I can stop one heart from breaking,

I shall not live in vain;

If I can ease one life from aching,

Or cool one pain,

Or help one fainting robin

Into his nest again,

I shall not live in vain.

~ Emily Dickinson

Letting Go

As humans, our brains are hard-wired to protect us and so we often struggle with letting go, with surrendering. Looking back I can see that at the time of Jacob's car accident I was most certainly not ready, willing, or able to let go of my child's life. But, as life moves on, our experiences expand our perspective and we gradually learn how and when to let go. I can recall the next big lesson I had in letting go was with a job I had been in for over 15 years. I had gone from being a volunteer to having a leadership position but the work environment became verbally and emotionally toxic. It was taking a tremendous toll on my health and I came to a realization that I had to get out to survive. That meant letting go of people and relationships and took several months of healing. However, I was beginning to understand the necessity of letting go of expectations; understanding that I could only control my decisions and responses. And yet, my most profound lesson of letting go was still to come. I can remember the moment when I realized that I would have to let go of my son's physical presence. As a mother that hurt every part of my being. I did not fully comprehend the power of his spiritual presence that would stay with me always.

Sometimes that presence shows up with a little bit of a wink. A couple years after his transition I had taken a trip with my husband to New Mexico where we discovered a connection between a Native American tribe there and his ancestry in El Paso. While there I purchased a beautifully handcrafted green malachite necklace. A year or so later I went looking for it to wear. It wasn't in my jewelry box. I looked everywhere I thought I could have possibly left it to no avail and gave it up, lost for good. Subsequently, a few years later, I was sitting in our living room watching television, which is in a large wooden cabinet with three sections that also hold our memorabilia of Jacob with his photo and the empty urn that is engraved with a honu, as well as photos and reminders of other family members who have transitioned and other mementos that connect to our ancestry. Out of the blue, I felt this nudge which made me look at his photo and it was as if he winked at me and said, “Mom, look in the honu box in the other cabinet.” There was a small box that had previously been sitting on my dresser, and lo and behold, there it was, my necklace! I immediately looked at his photo and said, “Thanks, son” and gave a little wink back.

“Take time to wonder at life and the world; see some humor in life where you can.” ~ Unknown

That wisdom has been revealed time and time again since his transition, and taught me the value of letting go, of surrendering, but in a way that is still full of hope. And I have come to understand that Love and Hope are verbs. These two words are not just “airy-fairy” feelings, they are words full of energy and motion (E+motion = emotion). They create physical and chemical changes in our bodies that are more powerful than we can imagine. Hope is belief with conviction and action.

In his book, *The Anatomy of Hope* (2004), Jerome Groopman, M.D., gives a documentation of what hope really is. Through his clinical study and personal experience, here are a few excerpts that helped me understand hope more fully.

"Hope can flourish only when you believe that what you do can make a difference…you are no longer entirely at the mercy of forces outside yourself," (p.26)

"...hope in the face of significant uncertainty…" (p.52)

"It is part of the human spirit to endure and give a miracle a chance to happen." (p. 81)

"Hope, then, is constructed not just from rational deliberation, from conscious weighing of information; it arises as an amalgam of thought and feeling, the feelings created in part by the neural input from the organs and tissues." (p.120)

And he concludes that *"Hope…is as vital to our lives as the very oxygen that we breathe."* (p.208)

My understanding of hope continued to expand as my caregiver roles changed. As I watched my parents and observed their illnesses separate them from their hope, this new wisdom helped me to see the traits that are necessary for us to survive and thrive through each caregiving journey.

In the following list, you may or may not feel completely connected to some, others that you feel you are still working on, and come to your own understanding that each of us expresses these traits in many different ways. As a caregiver we often overlook these traits, whether it be in celebrating what we have done or learning to build new skills.

Patience People who need care often take longer to complete simple tasks. As a caregiver, you might have to answer questions over and over. Good caregivers need patience to deal with anything from a loved one's memory lapses to angry outbursts. They practice staying calm and avoiding frustration.

Compassion Empathy and understanding are absolutely necessary. Even when they are caring for an abusive person, caregivers try to find balance and understanding.

Humor Finding something to laugh about can make a tough situation bearable. A sense of humor keeps a caregiver emotionally strong and is a great stress buster.

Being Present Good caregivers know the importance of respecting their loved one's current abilities. Rather than focus on what your loved one can no longer do, be in the moment with them. Look at photos, listen to music, cook a favorite meal. At the same time, remember that they weren't always sick.

Detail Oriented Good caregivers are good managers. They create schedules, plan for emergencies, and organize information so they don't have to scramble.

Able to Accept Help Asking for help is not a sign of weakness. A good caregiver realizes they can't do it all alone. They line up friends, family, or professionals to step in when they need a break.

Willing to Set Boundaries Respecting your limits, and saying no to demands, is an important trait.

Cooperative A good caregiver is part of a care team that may include doctors, family, and friends. Being understanding and flexible goes a long way toward being a successful team player.

Assertive Good caregivers advocate for their loved ones. They ask questions and expect answers. Good caregivers learn about their loved one's condition, and they make sure their loved one gets the care they need.

Fit Caregivers may make several trips up and down stairs every day. Others need to help their loved one move from bed to chair. Helping with these transfers can cause injury. Being strong isn't always enough to avoid hurting yourself. Caregivers need to know how to manage these chores safely (or get help).

In Good Health Taking care of your health might be the most important quality of a good caregiver. It's important to eat well, get enough sleep, and get regular exercise. Making and keeping your own doctor appointments is also key. And a good caregiver finds time to do something they enjoy. You can't take care of others well if you don't take care of yourself.

My new found awareness of letting go would continue to be put to the test as I became the caregiver for my parents. Again, my birth position put me in the place of being chosen and not necessarily choosing, to serve not just caring for them in physical ways, but also in medical and financial decision-making positions. One of the big letting go lessons would be in having to make the decision to move them to a care home and sell the house and most of their belongings to finance their care. By this time my father's Parkinson's was getting quite advanced and he was both physically and mentally challenged in his daily life. At the same time my mother was showing signs of dementia, and as she was trying to manage a household and her concern for my father, she was becoming quite anxious and agitated. Once my siblings and I all realized how critical both their physical and financial situation had become we had to make some quick decisions, one being to find a care home that we all felt comfortable with. We did not realize how challenging that would be. The options were limited and when we finally found one, only to be turned away, our second choice needed to be secured as quickly as possible or we would lose our space. This was followed with listing their house for sale and having an estate sale. My advice on this one is get help! Someone who understands the estate sale process and takes some of the emotional weight off your plate. It was especially hard for my father, who being an interior designer, was attached to a lot of their belongings. I am still not sure whether it was a blessing or a curse that we only had a month in which to make that all take place. But I did learn a valuable lesson in the art of decluttering and simplifying.

Painting of Laiki Place by Joan Fleming

I had spent my teenage years and my siblings most of their youth in this home that we now had to leave. We had moved there just before I entered eighth grade, and it was my father's dream home. Since he was an interior designer, our home became his personal showroom. He also loved to be with water, and we were less than a block away from what he called the biggest swimming pool on the planet—the Pacific Ocean. This is where my husband came to get me for our first date, and where we had our wedding reception. It was here that our children experienced holidays and their first birthday parties. It was filled with a lifetime of memories. It is still painful to remember my father wanting to keep going back, "one last time," to see if there was one more thing he might want to bring to the next place—a 12-foot square room. How could you possibly fit a lifetime in there? Several years later, the long anticipated moment of letting go of his physical life came upon us. He had made it clear that he did not want any kind of artificial support, and I am grateful that I was able to bring him back from the hospital to spend his last few breaths holding my mother's hand. Now, as I am writing this book, we are holding my mother's hand as she takes the very long and slow walk with dementia, knowing that soon we will need to let go. Letting go is not always easy, and yet learning this lesson helps us build resilience and perseverance in order to live a fulfilled life.

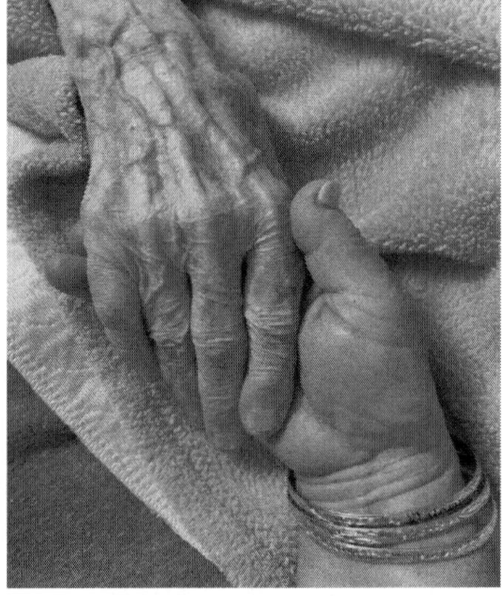

We All Learned to Let Go: Time in the time of COVID

In 2020 time took on a whole new meaning for the world when we realized we were facing a pandemic. I was just about to retire from the 9-to-5 work world, ready to slow down, so having to work from home for my last 30 days didn't seem so challenging. But not so for so many others. Not only did work spaces and schedules change, the fear of maybe not having employment at all was very real.

Next came the realization, and mandates, that we were to isolate ourselves. Humans are wired for connections from the time we are conceived. Scientific evidence has shown that babies who don't receive that human touch can fail to thrive, sometimes to the point where they end up passing away. The same is seen in the elderly who often become disconnected from family and loved ones. So, in order to keep some kind of human connection intact, we turned to technology and in some ways forgot the importance of that physical touch and how it helps us thrive.

As the days, months, and years went by, our concept or perception of time was both challenged and altered. We began to look at schedules with more fluidity. Rather than a 5-day/40-hour work week many have shifted to alternative work spaces and time constraints. This became evident in a conversation I had with a friend who was planning an online program and was considering two time frames—40 days or six weeks. In actual days it only differs by two, but the 40 days sounded so much more fluid, and in kairos time, than six weeks which seemed to feel more structured, constricted, and in chronos time. It seems to me that we had come to a time in our evolution where the Universe saw that we were out of balance in our doing and being, so had to give us a really good shake up. Now, it's a new day, and a new time, to find your way.

Lessons in Wisdom

"We are not human beings having a spiritual experience. We are spiritual beings having a human experience." ~ Pierre Teilhard de Chardin

---

Having experienced the birth of four children and witnessing the birth of a grandchild, having raised four children and witnessing the growth of countless others, I can say with certainty that we are created in and with Wisdom. We come into this world as part of that Divine Wisdom, and in our human experience we often have to lose some of it before it returns in its fullness.

Wisdom doesn't necessarily come with age but through moments and experiences in our lives. Although it sometimes takes years to fully understand its place, its value, its meaning. It is often in retrospect that the wisdom is revealed to us, and thus through that expansion of years and age it returns to that place where it began.

Wisdom can find its way back to us through many pathways, one of which is mentors. If you are fortunate to find these guides, pay close attention to their lessons of wisdom. And while finding your way back know that you also carry the responsibility, the kuleana, to share it with others. Another lesson of ALOHA.

Doing = Surviving, Being = Thriving. Along my journey the difference between the two became clearer and I chose to thrive.

In her book, *Thrive*, Arianna Huffington describes how it took a serious hit on the head (literally) to bring her to that awakening, and like her it was when my own health was being impacted by always living in the “doing” lane that I began to make decisions that moved me into the “being” lane. Also like her, I knew that if I was experiencing this need to change there were others who needed it too. And, her themes of well-being, wisdom, wonder, and giving aligned with my passion and purpose and with the values of ALOHA. A perfect fit!

Following His Footsteps

One of the most significant traveling experiences I have ever taken actually began as someone else's journey. In the fall of 2000, my son Jacob was involved with an exchange program with his high school and Spanish students. First the Spanish students came to Hawai'i and then the Hawai'i students went to Spain.

Jacob had been taking Spanish classes for over a year, but we really had no idea how much he knew or could articulate. We didn't speak it much at home, even though Spanish was my husband's first language. Our first indication that he knew more than we thought was during his exchange trip, and he called from a Western Union office in Madrid to ask us to send him more money. Evidently, he had been enjoying the company of more girls and dancing at more discos than we were aware of. The conversation between him and his father was in English, and then when he needed to sign for the money transfer, he quickly asked for "una pluma por favor," "a pen please". We quickly realized he was equipped enough to use it on command.

It wasn't until after his transition that we uncovered the journal he was required to keep on that trip. It was ALL written in Spanish. As we read through it, my husband and I decided that we wanted to retrace his steps with our own journey. From Hawai'i to Spain is a LONG TRIP! Over 36 hours of planes, trains, and automobiles to get to our first destination in Oviedo, which is in the north of Spain and that was where Jacob's trip had begun. Thank goodness I booked a five-star hotel for a good shower and a comfortable bed! Then on to Leon, Madrid, Toledo, Segovia, and Avila which were all on Jacob's itinerary.

Our senses were in overload! Familiar foods but with such a new experience. And the amazement of ancient architecture and history was fascinating. In Leon, the favorite food was the flan, made to perfection—so good I really was tempted to lick the plate. Next on the itinerary was Madrid. Our hotel was right near a central plaza where we shopped and ate several times in between our day tours to Toledo, Segovia, and Avila where we walked through time. Down cobblestone streets and through cathedrals that have existed for centuries.

All along the way we were mindful of those moments where we knew Jacob was walking with us. One was when a cat, looking almost exactly like his cat, Hampton, an ordinary tabby cat, was sitting outside a vendor's shop, as if to say, "See, I'm here." Another was a group of high school students taking the same tour as us, and one more was passing by the Western Union sign on one of our bus tours in Madrid and wondering if that was the one where he made that call. We also had the journal with us and continued to add to it with our own entries in Spanish. There are still blank pages in that journal yet to be filled.

A Tapestry of Life

From the day we are born our lives begin to stitch together a tapestry that often doesn't begin to be revealed until our later years, or sometimes even in our lifetime. When Jacob's diagnosis became terminal a good friend asked if she might initiate a quilt project for him. She asked that we send out an email notice to see who would want to participate and then she would send each person the instructions. First we were to choose from a selection of fabrics that she had collected that reflected his love of the ocean. Next each person was sent a blank piece of white cotton on which we were to draw a picture or message for him. Many of those that were received reflected that person's connection or relationship to Jacob. There were images of honu (turtles), koholā (whales), and ʻukulele, his favorite instrument. Others were stories—one about his biblical namesake and another of adventures with two of his best friends.

While he didn't have much time to use it, this quilt is our constant reminder of the rich tapestry of his twenty-two years. I now see life more as a tapestry and as it unfolds look closely for the colors, patterns, and golden threads of special memories and moments of my life.

Tattoos Tell a Story

It all started when our oldest son, Cielo, was turning 18, and my husband solemnly declared that there would be no tattoos or piercings allowed. So, first came just one ear piercing to which my husband commented something like, "So now you're a pirate?" Next stop, coming home from college for Christmas break, waiting for it to get noticed, with a small two-inch Christian fish symbol on one calf. It didn't take the youngest brother two seconds to see it immediately and Dad's comment this time was, "Did someone draw on your leg?" Well, that broke the dam. It was followed by the next two siblings getting tattoos as they turned 18, and the three older siblings taking the youngest for his first, which was the honu. Somewhere in those years, when I turned 50, I also took the plunge with my first tattoo, which was a butterfly to symbolize the transformation I felt I was taking—from doing to being.

Then came the big stories, again with our eldest leading the way with a full back tattoo representing his indigenous roots with the Aztec calendar. The middle son followed with a full back tattoo that represented his spiritual journey and included representation of many Hawaiian cultural images, such as the honu (green sea turtle) and koholā (humpback whale), which had also become spiritual representations of our family's journey. It was in Jacob's last few months before his transition that my husband finally relented, and told him that he would get the same honu tattoo that Jacob had, and on the same shoulder. I then had that same tattoo placed on my left thigh to connect with Jacob's car accident and followed that with four smaller versions as each grandchild was born. My husband's choice for the grandchildren was to have their Hawaiian names, given to them by our dear friend, Keale, tattooed in a piko (spiral/navel) design on his other shoulder. My culminating tattoo was when I turned 60 and is a five-inch honu/flower design on my right thigh. My tattoos are a reminder to walk with strength, integrity, and humility.

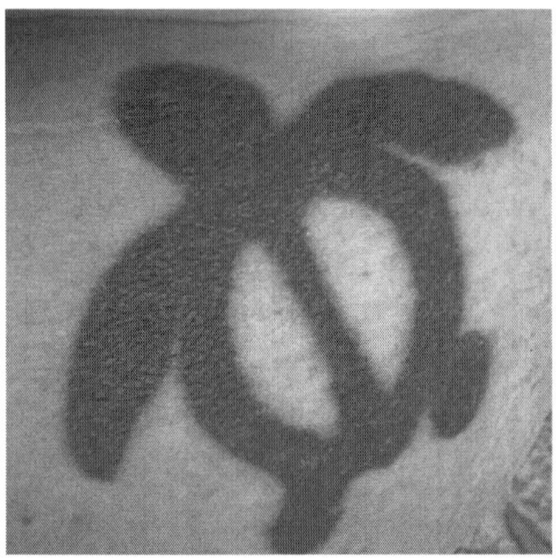

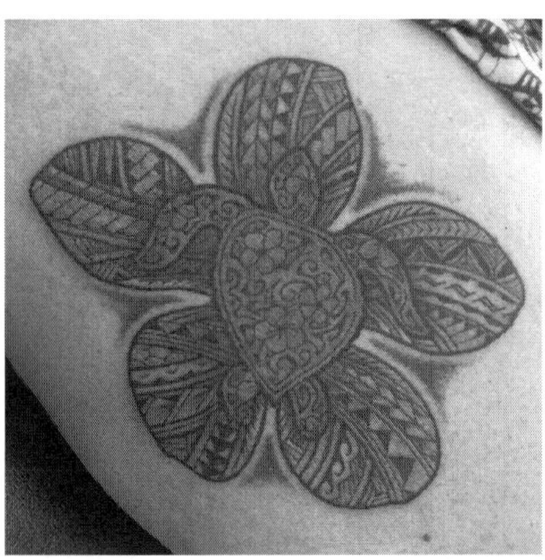

On the Other Side of Grief

"Grief ends up giving you the two best things: softness and illumination."

~ Anne Lamott, Traveling Mercies

In the first few months after Jacob's transition I discovered that as Westerners we have a lot to learn about processing our grief. I had many well-intentioned people say absolutely the wrong thing in their attempts to console me or advise me on how I should be grieving, and it all felt wrong. In my own attempts to move through the fog I found a book that shed light on the path to peace for my soul, *The Grief Recovery Handbook*, by John W. James. In this book, James writes about how when someone transitions all those close to them have each had a unique relationship with them and therefore each has their own unique journey through grief. It is not an orderly process of sequential steps. It is often uneven and unordered. And it isn't something that you get over, it is something you learn to live with, that you grow into and around. In that understanding, all of our immediate family was able to give each other the time and space we needed to move through the heaviness of it all to a place of peace. It brought us all to a new spiritual awareness and created a special bond that holds our family together as new descendants come and ancestors move on. We also gained a clearer understanding of our need to care for our health and well-being. To bring more of the being into the doing of our lives.

Observations speak volumes even as words fall short. While I don't remember ever having had conversations with my husband and children about doing and being, I have witnessed it, especially in the last weeks of Jacob's transition. At the time they were all adults beginning the busy doing of their lives, and yet I saw that they had to stop and be present in that experience. Our oldest son had to stop his military service, our daughter had to stop her teaching, and our next son had to stop his studies at seminary. That time seemed to create a new awareness for them on finding the balance of doing and being. As their lives have moved on I have seen them struggle to keep that balance, as we all do. Those being moments of transition, whether it be in death or birth, require us to be more present mentally, emotionally, and spiritually. These are the moments where the doing disappears.

So, once we have that awareness, how do we maintain a balance of doing and being going forward? It begins with cultivating those daily habits that will become your foundation. A firm, solid, unshakeable foundation. Small steps taken over and over again that lead you and sustain you on whatever course your life journey might take.

Be mindful about what you consume. This applies to mind, body, and spirit. Be intentional about your consumption of media and read more of what helps reinforce the being mindset. Be intentional about what you put into your body with nutritional foods and hydration. Be intentional about finding the spiritual guidance that keeps you mindful.

Maintaining the balance also comes with surrounding yourself with a community of support. It is said we become like the five people we spend the most time with so it's imperative to choose wisely. And, be sure you are one of those positive people that supports you. You can accomplish that with daily I AM affirmations.

Alaka'i Lesson - I AM

The path may not always be smooth, but by implementing all of these daily habits, it helps to keep your doing/being in balance especially on the rockiest parts of the journey.

Sometimes in the doing we need to separate ourselves from the emotions of being. In the years after Jacob's passing my caregiving role with parents began to increase. My father's Parkinsons was advancing and my mother's Alzheimers was in its early stages. They were still living independently so I would stop by in the morning on my way to work and then back again after work to check on them. It became evident that we needed additional help. I realized that I could not sustain the being of me while I was in the doing of caring for my parents. That eventually led to moving them to a care home. One of my dad's wishes for end of life care was absolutely no artificial means of life support and to him that included any type of tubes or needles. His last trip to the hospital was because he was having congestive heart failure and he kept fighting the doctors attempts to suction out his lungs, and said to me, "You lied." I knew that he was referring to the tubes and needles. And while those words stung, it was also the day I realized I was not responsible for my parents' suffering. I reassured him that if he could calm down enough to be transported I would get him back "home". We did and within 30 minutes of being back in his bed, holding my mother's hand, he took his last breath.

Under My Kukui Tree

Trees have captured the human imagination for centuries. Their lore is found in many cultures and in some cases they are a source for worship. There is a sense that trees are much like us as humans, rooted to the earth, with limbs that are meant to embrace. They share the same Earth energy and air with us and in many cases provide us shelter and protection that are so important to our spiritual existence. It is no wonder that we can feel so connected.

The kukui tree in my backyard has been one of the main sources of enlightenment for my journey with Alaka'i Associates. It began as a sapling carried down from the Ko'olau mountains and given to us by our friend, Walt. It sat in its pot for several years, patiently waiting for us to tend to it. Every time we happened to notice it, it would have one or two little green leaves to tell us it was hanging on. Then, as it happens, we had cut down an old coconut tree and had the roots mulched so we thought that might be a good place to try to plant our kukui tree. It was a perfect spot, as the tree began to grow rapidly, and within just a couple of years was big enough to provide shade and became a perfect place for meditation.

Now it embraces our family as well. I truly believe that there is a Universal energy source in every part of creation and if we stop and listen it has wisdom to share with us.

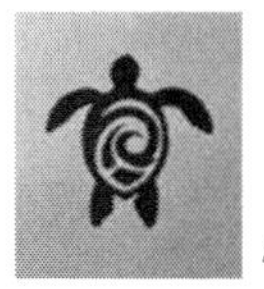

Alaka'i Lesson - Be A Tree Meditation

Coincidence or God-incident

Coincidence - life happens to me: God-incident - life happens for me

Years ago a friend introduced me to this unique play on words; coincidence or God-incident, and it helped me reframe how I saw the world. Now, in the context of this book it appears to me that one reflects more on doing and the other on being. When we see life as a string of coincidences we often don't stop to consider their meaning. We are temporarily surprised or entertained by the serendipitous moment, but it is soon forgotten. When we are able to shift our perspective to those events having some divine direction we are likely to be viewing it from a being mindset. Ever since I was awakened to this small, yet significant, difference, those moments never escape me. As I look back I can see times where I may have missed that divine connection, but that all changed because of Jacob's transition. Even as that was unimaginably hard, I now look for and anticipate those wonderful God-incidents and know that life is happening for me.

Here's how I know this is true…

I had big plans for my retirement in 2020, the Universe had other plans. I was ready to launch into my new wellness business endeavors by facilitating a three-day retreat. The venue was secured, all the supplies purchased, and then Covid came along and shut it down. While I was a little upset with having to put everything on pause, I took it as a sign that I needed to really sit in the "being" space for a while. In the months that followed I tried my hand at gardening (not my forte, although I do enjoy feeling the earth in my hands), went on mini excursions with my husband just to sight-see, and continued writing my blog. Then, in 2021, a string of those "God-incidents" began to come together. I reconnected with an acquaintance, who then introduced me to a new acquaintance, and at that first meeting I found where my passion and purpose would come together. I met the founder of a new nonprofit that was caring for caregivers. I knew that space, I had lived in that space, and I had what they needed—how to find the balance in the chaos of the doing and being of caregiving.

Part III: ALAKA'I LIFE LESSONS

All the lessons of a lifetime have brought me to this place, this new chapter of my life. And perhaps you are there too. So, how do you sustain your vision for growth? How do you keep focused on self care? How do you find calm in chaos?

In this last section, you will find some of my lessons, meditations, and simple strategies for leading a more balanced life in the midst of the yin and yang of doing and being.

It all starts and ends with gratitude.

The Art of Being in Gratitude and Abundance

I came to an awareness that abundance comes in many forms and we have to train ourselves to notice it. Somewhere along my path I became keenly aware of how expressing gratitude on a daily basis could alter the journey ahead in a positive way. Practice and fortitude brings us into being with gratitude and abundance. It paves the path with smooth stones that would protect us from falling.

My daily prayer has become, "I am grateful for the abundance I have received; I am grateful for the abundance I am about to receive; and I am grateful for the abundance I am able to share." That daily practice is part of the art of being.

I remember a moment when I was trying to visualize how my Alaka'i business would evolve and saw clearly in my mind the image of a large Asian style fishing basket. They are usually about two feet in diameter and very shallow. What I saw was the basket filling with abundance in both health and wealth for me personally but then as it continued to fill would overflow and that was the abundance I was able to share with others. I went on an extensive search to find just the right basket. It took several months but once I found it I had to get it, even though it seemed a bit pricey. To this day the basket holds space in my office as a reminder to keep my life filled to overflow with gratitude and good works.

Reflection: Do you have a daily practice of gratitude?

Breathe

I remember that pivotal moment in learning the power of breath and breathing. As humans we are wired to survive and when we feel threatened, fear can cause us to hold our breath. But at some point we must come up for air and sometimes are gasping for it.

That first critical moment was when Jacob was hit by the car in front of our house. I saw it about to happen and by the time I was out the door he was lying in the street. As I rushed to him a neighbor gently stepped in front of me, held my shoulders and quietly said, "Take a breath."

In the 30-plus years since that moment there have been many more times when crises or fear have taken my breath away. But along the way I have come to realize that even in our daily lives the stressors can cause us to hold our breath. Unknowingly, when we tense up, and are not breathing fully or deeply, we are depriving our bodies of the oxygen it needs to function at its full capacity. Learning breathing techniques has led me to a new awareness of this critical function and I have incorporated it into my daily habits and support resources.

Two of my favorites are the Teardrop and the Square because they can be visualized easily and even drawn out on paper.

> For the Teardrop, start at the top and inhale as you move to the bottom expansion, then begin to exhale as you move back up to the top.

For the Square, imagine a square or have a visual in front of you. Begin at the lower right corner and go up and inhale to the count of four, then across the top of the square as you hold to the count of four, then down the right side and exhale to the count of four, and finally across the bottom as you hold to the count of four.

The Square is great for calming as it brings balance to your breathing.

As I began to incorporate these techniques into my daily habits and meditation practices I found that it is often recommended that you do them in sets of three, sometimes called cleansing breaths, and wondered about that significance. In part, it connects with the emotional components of the stress cycle, and in part to help side-step the serious "self-improvement" mindset that just creates more things to do. These three breaths have been described in this way: The first breath, the Centering Breath, can calm and soothe your body and give you a sense of control over your response; the second breath, the Possibility Breath, can restore the tranquility of your mind and allow you to perceive your highest choices; and the third breath, the Discovery Breath, can reunite you with your spirit and turn a stressful situation into a learning opportunity.

Reflection: When, where, and how will you create moments to breathe?

"Feelings come and go like clouds in a windy sky. Conscious breathing is my anchor." ~ Thich Nhat Hanh

"You are where you need to be. Just take a deep breath." ~ Lana Parilla

Looking at Time with a Different Lens

In those days of doing and trying to "manage" my time I came across a book that helped me shift my perspective to "mapping" my time instead. In her book, *Time Management from the Inside Out,* Julie Morgenstern helps you take that elusive entity of time and create a more visual, creative, and tangible way of seeing it and making the most of it.

Here is how I put her "time mapping" strategies into practice:

- First, write out your big dreams and goals. It really is the first part of mapping - you have to know where you are going. When you want to use the navigation system in your car or on your phone it knows where you are starting but you have to plug in the destination. Yes, there might be detours, but if you have that goal firmly locked in, your own navigation system will be able to make the adjustments.
- Next step is to be sure to include the small stops along the way. What are the priorities that you want to keep while on this journey? Self, family, work, finances, community, knowledge. How much time do you want to spend in each area, and how much time are you currently spending in each area?
- Now, you can begin to plan your "rest stops". Ask yourself, "Am I doing my activities at the right time for me?" "Does my schedule make me feel balanced and energized?"

- Keep doing this exercise until you can confidently say yes to each step.

One way to do this is to have some type of planner, but again be sure it fits your preferences. Are you a visual/tactile person or more linear? What size best suits your needs? Over the years I have used a variety of methods depending on the work I was doing but the one non-negotiable, that I never waiver from, is creating my "white space", the time between activities where I can bring mind, body, and spirit back together before moving on to the next activity.

Reflection: Are you managing or mapping your time?

Creating White Space

Remember that datebook that went flying off the back of the car? Well as I continued my journey as a mother, wife, student, and professional every time slot in that planner was full, or at least it felt full. There didn't seem to be time for self care—you know the simple things like eating healthy, exercising, and sleeping. There might have been good intentions but it really wasn't part of my daily habits. It wasn't until my 50's (and trust me when I say don't wait that long) when I was at a work retreat with a small group of women when I had the aha moment. We were doing an activity creating identity boards, which are much like a vision board but using pictures and words to depict ourselves, our lives, our aspirations. By then I had done many vision boards and goal posters, and most times they were a collage of everything overlapping to cover the whole page. This time was different. I found myself deliberately leaving space between each portion of my life—family, work, me. When we were done and sharing with the group one of the women asked me why there was so much "white space." I realized that in the months before I had been deliberately creating space in my calendar by trying not to schedule meetings back-to-back. I would try to give myself 15-30 minutes so that I could transition and bring my mind, body, and spirit back together and be able to show up for the next one with a greater sense of presence and awareness. This practice has become one of the self care and stress management habits I teach.

Reflection: Where do you find or create white space?

Transformation Strategies

The butterfly has long been seen as a symbol for transformation and change and seems mystical and magical. But if you really study the process of that change you will find that it resembles much of how we as humans experience major life changes.

Stage One is that "dissolving", or falling apart, because that change is often unexpected and we are unprepared. Some strategies for getting through this stage are:

- Live one day at a time. (or sometimes just minutes at a time) Focus on the here and now.
- Actually, "cocoon" yourself. Wrap yourself in your favorite blanket, have a soothing cup of tea. Do what feels comforting.
- Find someone to talk to—a friend or therapist. Someone who will be reassuring.
- Let yourself grieve. Yes, through all major changes, we experience a sense of loss. Let yourself experience those emotions. Acknowledging them will help you move through this stage.

Stage Two is the metamorphosis, in that liquid substance, are these *imago* cells that contain all the instructions for the creation of the butterfly. This is where we can begin to see what the life ahead of us might look like. To encourage that imaginative thinking, you might want to:

- Start a discovery journal or vision board. Cut out pictures you find interesting and appealing and let them begin to illustrate the life you are trying to create.
- You can also start a written journal of your dreams, schemes, and aspirations— planning to bring your vision to fruition.

Stage Three is reforming. This is where you stop dreaming and start implementing. Your vision starts to take shape and become more substantive. Sometimes, this stage needs repeating as you continue to re-form and refine your new life.

- Expect there to be some failures and be willing to start over.
- Persist and persevere.

Stage Four is emerging. As you leave the stage of reforming you are like the butterfly just emerging from the cocoon. Don't rush that stage, as like the butterfly, you must let your newly formed soggy wings have a chance to dry and strengthen before you are ready to fly.

- Be patient.
- Enjoy your new existence.
- Spend time every day focusing on gratitude.
- Find small ways to add pleasure to your life.

And now you know that the next time change occurs, and it will, you have the skills to make it through.

Reflection: When have you had a transformative experience?

Cultivating Calm out of Chaos

Over the years I have written and rewritten this list, each time to remind myself that I can thrive even in the midst of surviving. So here goes, in no particular order:

Breathe—deeply and often.

Keep it simple.

Cultivate gratitude.

Don't overschedule.

Allow an extra half hour for everything you do.

Drink lots of water.

Move—walk, dance, run.

Laugh more often.

Let Mother Nature nurture.

Stop trying to please everyone.

Start pleasing yourself.

Nurture friendships.

Don't be afraid of your passion.

Set goals and surrender expectations.

Care for your soul.

Cherish your dreams.

Express love everyday.

Be instead of do.

Reflection: Copy this list, or create your own. Write it somewhere that you can come back to it to cultivate that calm space.

Discovery Journal

One of the earliest habits that I can recall developing was keeping a journal and over the years, while the content or format may have changed, it is an anchor to my day. One of the first journals I started was with *The Simple Abundance Journal of Gratitude*. Like most people I wasn't sure how to start and so I was grateful that this journal gave you a whole list of prompts to keep me going. Here are a few I chose from the list that were relative to where my life was at the time: Grateful for the moment of relief when the migraine pain had subsided; not having to cook one night; a nap; summoning up the courage to surmount a challenge:resigning from a toxic job; letters from my oldest son at military boot camp; notes for affirmation to follow my goals and dreams from colleagues and family. Start with just three things to be grateful for, either to start or end your day, and overtime see how it impacts your mind, body, and spirit.

One of my favorite tools is what I call a Discovery Journal. It is a combination of several different resources I have used over the years such as photo journals, writing journals, goal posters, and vision boards. I create them with a composition notebook—blank or lined—and first fill the cover with pictures and affirmations. They become great visualization tools and can be created for a number of different purposes. So, let's focus on visualization for a moment. It can be so powerful in creating the life you want.

Reflection: Where does your discovery begin?

A Peaceful Place

Visualization is a great place to start building those daily habits. My understanding of the power of visualization came when Jacob was going through his radiation treatments. Because he had a brain tumor he had to have a mesh mask made that was locked into place over his head each time he had a treatment. It can be very claustrophobic and create a lot of stress. As part of the patient support at this hospital they had someone who would work with the patients on creating a visualization of a safe and peaceful place they could go to while being locked under that mask. One day I asked Jacob if he would share his visualization with me and it has become one of my favorite peaceful places.

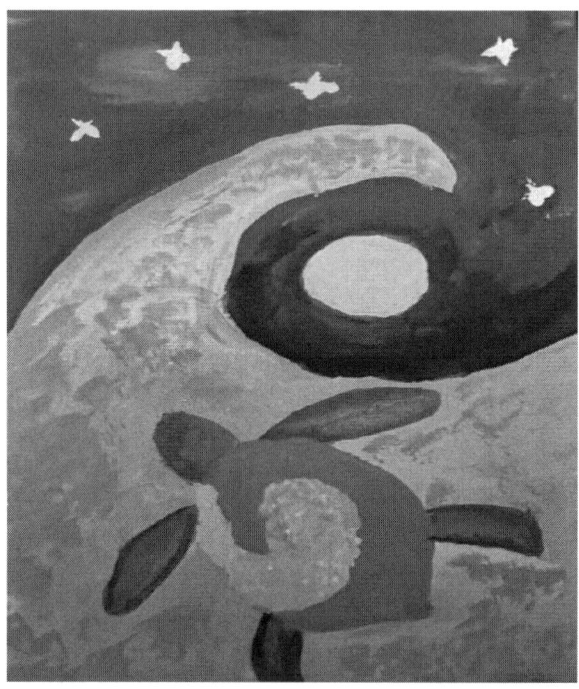

Imagine this: Have you ever seen a full moon coming up over the horizon, casting its light across the water? Now imagine that you are riding on the back of a giant honu (sea turtle) right through that light on the water. Do you feel the movement of the waves? Can you smell the sea? What do you hear? I could stay out there forever!

Reflection: Where would your visualization take you?

The Power of Our Senses

In one of my favorite meditations you are guided through the rooms of your five senses - plus one more, your sixth sense, your inner vision. In doing this meditation, I am reminded of how powerful our senses are, especially our sense of smell. It is one of the most miraculous ways that we experience the world around us. Even faint aromas can engage our sense of smell and trigger an emotional response. While the way that our brain processes aromas is somewhat complex, there is a simple explanation as to how a specific smell can elicit a response within us.

Indulge me with this little science lesson.....

Our sense of smell starts with the olfactory system which is the part of the brain that controls our sense of smell. When an aroma reaches the nostrils the molecules are detected by olfactory receptors. Once detected they send signals to the brain to be identified. That information is transmitted to the limbic system, which is the part of the brain where our emotions and memories are stored, and creates a response based on emotions and memories that have been associated with that particular aroma. However, because some aromas have specific chemical compounds that are known to produce a general type of response,like uplifting or calming,it is possible to harness the power of smell to elicit a desired response. Okay, the science lesson is done.

Every time I do this meditation I recall memories associated with smells and while there are a few unpleasant ones, most trigger wonderful associations. For instance, petrichor, the smell of rain that sends out the aromas of earth and woods. Or the smell of a fresh pumpkin pie baking that brings back memories of happy holidays. And then there is one particular unpleasant aroma that is connected to a funny memory. As a young child we would often visit my paternal grandparents in western Nebraska. I recall on one occasion riding with my grandfather on the interstate and being stuck behind a large rig transporting cattle. As you might imagine the aroma wafting back to us was rather potent. I must have made some derogatory remark, like "pee yew" or "that stinks" and being the good mid-Westerner and banker that he was, he replied, "Nope. Honey, that's the smell of money." It's still not my favorite aroma but reminds me of one of my favorite people.

Reflection: Take some time to notice the smells that trigger memories for you and be grateful for that miraculous gift.

"Be a Tree" Meditation

This meditation is designed to help you get in touch with the oneness of nature and to assist you in finding personal stability, harmony, and balance.

Close your eyes and take three deep, relaxing breaths right into the core of your belly and exhale them gently through the cells of your entire body. Watch your belly expand as you breathe in and your body open and relax as you breathe out.

Breathe in. Breathe out. Notice the sounds of nature around you. Peaceful. Inviting. Visualize a magnificent tree before you. Hear it whisper something to you as you approach it. Feel the texture and smell the fragrance of the tree.

Now with one deep relaxing breath, allow yourself to merge into the center of the majestic tree, and in your imagination, rise to enable your body to gracefully fill the trunk of the tree.

Feel your feet, legs and the base of your spine sinking deep, deep, deep into Mother Earth down, down into the moist, dark ground to become one strong and stable taproot. Watch as your feet and legs branch out to create a far-reaching labyrinth of finer roots.

Your head stretches and expands to occupy a dynamic space amongst the foliage, and you feel a whole new level of perfect clarity and acute perception. Your hands and arms rise as they transform into many strong and intricate branches. Watch as vibrant leaves sprout on your network of branches and twigs reaching into the sky.

Sublime cosmic forces and information enter your being. Become aware that you are a conduit of light, absorbing sunlight and starlight. As you anchor this light into the ground, know that you are literally anchoring heaven on earth.

Stretch your entire being luxuriously and fully inhabit your new identity as a dignified tree. Feel your perfect balance, stability, and harmony. Be flexible like the tree in the wind. Observe how it feels to stand strong yet supple like the tree.

Now experience the life within and around you. Notice what is occurring throughout your entire system. Begin at the tips of your roots and work up to your trunk and then into your branches, twigs, and leaves. Feel your essence and presence.

Tune in to the interplay of all your aspects and to your connectedness within yourself and the world around you. Become aware of other trees and how you communicate with them. You are a reservoir of wisdom and have many lessons to teach and stories to tell. Each tree ring is a year's storehouse of growth with every full cycle of the sun. Tap into the knowledge archived in each of your rings.

What do you teach of the changing of the seasons, of the gifts of abundance, of giving and receiving, sheltering, patience, beauty, freedom, mystery, and generosity to visitors over the years of your life?

Observe all the life forms that you shelter and nourish—birds, bugs, bees, butterflies and other insects and wildlife. Listen to the harmonious sounds of life within and around you.

Feel the spirit of your tree. Tune into tree consciousness. Identify the feeling. How long has your tree resided here? What is it capable of? What does it know?

Listen deeply within. There is profound ancient wisdom in this tree. It has a personal message for you. What does it want you to know? Take some time to fully absorb this message. Now thank the tree for all its gifts.

When you are ready, slowly withdraw your consciousness back from every part of the tree. Draw yourself out of the roots. Come back up from the ground, and back from the branches, leaves, and trunk. Allow the tree to send you safely back into your body—back home to yourself. Return fully and totally into your body.

Breathe naturally and begin to move. Notice the sounds around you and become aware of your breathing. Recall your personal message from the tree and reflect upon it.

Open your eyes and gently complete your meditation.

Reflection: Where do you find and feel most grounded?

The Principles of Attitudinal Healing

- ★ The essence of our being is love.
- ★ Health is inner peace. Healing is letting go of fear.
- ★ Giving and receiving are the same.
- ★ We can let go of the past and of the future.
- ★ Now is the only time there is and each instant is for giving.
- ★ We can learn to love ourselves and others by forgiving rather than judging.
- ★ We can become love finders rather than fault finders.
- ★ We can choose and direct ourselves to be peaceful inside regardless of what is happening outside.
- ★ We are students and teachers to each other.
- ★ We can focus on the whole of life rather than the fragments.
- ★ Since love is eternal, death need not be viewed as fearful.
- ★ We can always perceive ourselves and others as either extending love or giving a call for help.

Reflection: Where and how can you apply these principles to your life?

14 Day Mindset Reset

It is sometimes hard to recognize the effects of stress, even when it has been in a time of celebration, and when you are a caregiver it can seem compounded. It can be difficult to determine whether the worst part of stress is its source—work issues, family problems, or keeping up with a house that is in constant need of cleaning or fixing; OR the effects on your health and wellness with tight muscles, anxiety, or sleeplessness.

Here is a "prescription" to take back your mind, body, and spirit – fourteen days to find your inner calm, in and out of chaos.

Day 1: *Survey your support system.* I call this my "Lifeboat". Make a list of the people you could turn to for advice and a helping hand. Knowing that they are there can make you feel more resilient.

Day 2: *Plant something.* Even if it is just a small pot of herbs for your kitchen. Studies show that gardening can help shift the focus away from stressors and give you a sense of calm.

Day 3: *Take a break.* Have a cup of tea. Regularly drinking black tea can lower stress hormones and induce feelings of relaxation. (*This is one I can easily remember! I love tea!*)

Day 4: *Get a massage.* A short 15-minute shoulder or foot massage can chip away at accumulated stress and calm your nerves. Even a quick hand massage can help – press your thumb and forefinger of one hand between the fleshy part of your hand between your thumb and forefinger on the other hand. Hold for 60 seconds.

Day 5: *Get distracted*. Play solitary games like solitaire or sudoku, or do crossword puzzles. Find one that you really like so that you become so absorbed you lose track of time. (*I turn off my devices an hour before bed and do crossword puzzles*.)

Day 6: *Be grateful*. Make a list of three to five specific things you are grateful for. When you focus on the good in your life it flips a switch in your brain and stress will recede. Make this a daily practice.

Day 7: *Think Pink*. Research has shown that a bubble gum shade of pink has a soothing effect so add a little pink to your wardrobe or your office. It can be as easy as using light pink Post-it notes.

Day 8: *Take a Drive*. When you can, change your commute to take a more scenic route to or from work. This will give you a chance to either set your thoughts for the day or unwind on the way home.

Day 9: *De-tangle Yourself.* Make a point to stand up and stretch if you have been sitting for more than 45 minutes. *(You can set a reminder on your phone or computer to stand up.)* Consciously release the tension that has built up in your neck, shoulders, back, etc. And, BREATHE! Deep inhalations through your nose and exhalations through your mouth.

Day 10: *Lend a Hand*. Reaching out to someone else in need gets you away from your own worries and can often put things in perspective to make you feel better about your own circumstances.

Day 11: *Laugh a Little*. The minute you start laughing your body turns on the feel-good endorphins and provides oxygen to boost your mood. And laughing with someone doubles the dose.

Day 12: *Turn off the Tube*. TV's constant bombardment of information can add to feelings of anxiety so give yourself a night off. Find a more relaxing visual or aural stimulation – like reading or listening to music.

Day 13: *Put up a Stop Sign*. When stressful thoughts start creeping in, visualize holding up a bright red stop sign. Take a few deep breaths and decide your next turn. Turn towards a more positive thought.

Day 14: T*here is a Bigger Plan*. As problems arise, ask yourself, "Will this matter in three months? Three years?" Try to see the bigger picture and take small steps to a better outcome.

Reflection: When, where, and how did you see or feel a shift in your mindset?

Aging in Wellness

Whether we admit it or not, we do start aging the day we are born and those physical changes begin to escalate as early as our twenties. Wait, don't stop reading now! There is good news! Between ancient healing modalities and modern science we are uncovering new ways to age in wellness and not in illness. But, I am getting ahead of my story.

In those busy adult "doing years" I paid some attention to being healthy and trying to provide a healthy environment for my family, but I must admit it wasn't always at the top of my priority list. I remember very clearly when it was brought to my attention that I was definitely in the aging process.

As my educational and professional career grew so did the use of technology and my eyes' exposure to new stress and strain. I had been wearing glasses off and on for most of my life, so I went in for an eye exam. I explained to the doctor that I was sure any changes were due to my work environment and was a little taken aback when he looked at my chart and said, very matter-of-factly, "Well, that's to be expected with you turning 40." What?! Who said anything about age?! How rude! Moving on...

Then there's the next big milestone—50. Now, I start noticing how the aging process is affecting my overall health with weight, sleep, and more. It's time to take action and this is where I began to develop my strategies for self care and stress management.

Another decade goes by and while retirement is on the horizon I feel like I have a whole new opportunity to get it right and understand how to age in wellness and not in illness, and share that wisdom with the world through Alaka'i Associates. And, here we are! So, whether you are twenty-five, forty-five, sixty-five, or eight-five, let's continue this journey together.

In those years, moving from doing to being, I was fortunate to have the opportunity to work with the *Blue Zones* project as it was being introduced in Hawaii, and as I was growing in my awareness of wellness. The *Power of 9** principles of the Blue Zones fell into alignment with my vision for my own health journey, and for my mission with Alaka'i Associates to help others lead healthier lives, so I began to incorporate those principles into both my personal and professional life.

Here's how:

Move naturally. I began a walking routine and find it provides a perfect balance between doing and being.

Purpose. Using the concept of "ikigai" I was able to find clarity in combining my passion and purpose to bring Alaka'i to life. Ikigai is, above all else, a lifestyle that strives to balance the spiritual with the practical. This balance is found at the intersection where your passions and talents converge with the things that the world needs and is willing to pay for. It is the intersection of passion and purpose and is supported by a close circle of friends.

Down Shift. This one takes some considerate effort when moving from a doing to being perspective. For me it began with three down shift times during my day - morning meditation, midday hydration, evening gratitude.

80% Rule. Beginning with this simple awareness, that there are healthier alternatives to the way we eat. We don't need to super-size anything or clean the plate. Start with a smaller plate.

Plant Slant. I started by making a few changes and just kept going. I even grew some of my own! But now I rely on my local farmers' market.

Wine @5. The most important part is the time spent with others in this end of day wind-down. And if wine is part of that, there is a value to limiting the amount of any alcohol to two glasses a day.

Belong. This is a basic need for all humans and is often connected to a faith community of some kind. One of my favorite quotes is that we are not just human beings having a spiritual experience, but actually spiritual beings having a human experience. That spirituality is what makes us all one.

Loved ones first. This one has become quite a challenge in our ever-growing and moving communities. So even if you can't keep your aging relatives with you, keep connected to them as much as possible.

Right Tribe. Remember my Lifeboat Theory? That's my tribe. The Okinawans probably do it best with their moai which are groups of five people who are committed to each other for life. Our social networks have an impact on our capacity to age in wellness.

The wisdom of ancestors and cultures from around the world affirmed that there are universal truths that can guide us to age in wellness and not in illness.

Reflection: Which one of the Power9 will you start with today?

A Plan for Wellness

In a quote from the book *The E Myth* by Michael Gerber, he says, “Entrepreneurs who fail work *IN* their business, not *ON* their businesses.” The same goes for our lives! Most of us are too busy. We are rushing to do ‘things’ all the time, working, caregiving, being with family, housework, going out socially, studying, and generally feeling overwhelmed the vast bulk of the time. We are working **IN** our lives and not taking time out to work **ON** our lives!

Here is a guide to setting up a plan to work **ON** your life, restore your JOY, create some balance and find energy! As you go through this activity you will know where the imbalances are, and how to restore some balance.

Find yourself some paper or a journal to create your Plan For Wellness. Create a separate page for each segment and write the segment name at the top of the page; and draw a 0-10 scale next to it.

- Leisure/Relaxation (ie: 0 --------------------- 10)
- Family
- Spirituality
- Intimate Relationships
- Health
- Friendship
- Work

Attention AND Importance

Now comes the reflection time! Look at one page at a time—at that one aspect of your life and mark it 0 if you put no attention on it at all and 10 if you are doing well at it. Write about why you are where you are on the scale of 0-10.

Next, go back through the sections and rate them on a scale of 0-10 of importance. If you have an area that you believe is really important to you but you place no or little attention on it—what impact do you think it will have on you? Again, write out your thoughts.

A lot of unconscious stress comes about when we are:

1. not conscious of how we feel;
2. unaware of the imbalances in each area;
3. don't have a plan or commitment to address those imbalances.

For example, if you look at Leisure/Relaxation where would you be on the attention scale? Do you pay attention to you and your needs? Do you give yourself time on a regular basis to just stop? Time to stop and breathe and relax completely? To focus on you and how you are feeling? To work out why you are feeling a certain way and decide what would make you feel better? Now, decide how important you are to *you*! How important is it to you to take care of yourself? To renew your spirit? If you are not putting much attention on you and your leisure time—socializing, having fun, or just connecting with others—AND you place little importance on it, what does that tell you about you? And how do you feel about yourself? Taking time out to recover and renew your physical, mental, spiritual and emotional wellbeing is a necessity, not a luxury. It needs to rank at about 10 on the scale of importance!

Given where you are now in both attention and importance, where would you like to be on those scales instead? Jot that down. What do you need to do to reach those numbers? How do you have to think differently? What beliefs do you need to address? What specific commitments will you make to yourself to give yourself the time and attention you need—and to give yourself permission that you are more important than perhaps housework for three hours!

It reminds me of the instructions flight attendants give prior to takeoff. They say something to the effect of, “Should anything happen while in flight, oxygen masks will fall from the ceiling.” If you are with a child, what do they tell you to do? Put the oxygen mask on yourself first! Why? Because if you can’t breathe you are not much use to the child!! You need to take care of yourself so you can take care of others when you need to! *It’s important AND it deserves attention!*

Do the same with the other areas. Rank yourself on the scale of 0-10 for both the amount of attention you place on it, and how important it is to you. Take note of those that rank low in both importance and attention, and those where you rank high in importance but low on the amount of attention you put on it.

The ones that rank low are the primary ones to begin to work on. Decide where you would like to be in each area on both scales, and then start a plan. We are the ones in charge of our wellness, our joy, our experience of life! We, more than anyone, can influence our own state of mind, and heart, and physical health with our choices and decisions. Becoming aware of where we are on the wellness scale is the start. Your Plan For Wellness gives you specific areas to address and the way to get there!

Reflection: Have you made a plan for self care and wellbeing?

High Fives

Here's an exercise to begin and end your day: High Five Your Heart

Place your own hand on your own heart, so that you feel the warm touch of your hand on your heart center.

Breathe gently, softly, deeply into your heart center.

If you wish, breathe in a sense of ease or safety or goodness into your heart center.

Then remember one moment, just one moment, when you felt safe, loved, and cherished by another human being. Not the entire relationship, just one moment. This could be a partner or child, a friend or therapist or teacher; it could be a spiritual figure; it could be a pet.

As you remember this moment of feeling safe and loved and cherished, let yourself feel deeply into the feeling of that moment. Let the feeling wash through your body, and let yourself stay there for 20 or 30 seconds. Notice any shifts in your sense of relaxation and calm.

Reflection: How, when and where will you begin to use this practice?

Your Golden Ember

(photo of nature mandala made of kukui tree pieces, created at Moanalua Valley, 2022)

Here is a short meditation to help you focus on your light, your spark, your ember.

Begin by following your breath….Experience the rhythm of the in-breath and the out-breath….Allow your mind to settle into your breath….Be aware of thoughts that arise but don't try to do anything about them….They will arise, and go away.

Imagine a small golden light in your heart center, a golden flame….Feel its warmth….Imagine this as the light of awareness, that guiding presence that is always with us….Continue to be aware of your breath, but also of that light in your heart….Let yourself rest in it....Trust that there is a light within you that knows you, reveals yourself to you, and guides you.

Slowly breathe that light out into the world....Imagine that it travels far....activating light and awareness wherever it goes....Know that as you sit quietly in and with that light you are awakening it in the vast network of consciousness, of which we are all a part....Ask that all beings experience the light of awareness within them....Know that as you arise from this meditation, that light goes with you.

Believe there is a loving Source.

Reflection: How will you keep your golden ember burning?

I AM

There have been several times over the span of my adult life where I have been asked to do an exercise with the statement, "I am" that often includes many of the roles we identify with throughout our life. As I was looking through my files and notes in this writing process I uncovered one that was different. It took me back over twenty-five years to a college communication course. I immediately recalled the lecture hall and professor who gave us the assignment. She simply wrote "I…" on the board and gave us one minute to write as many words as we could to describe "I" without using roles or titles. Here's my list:

I…

Eternal

Divine

Love

Grace

Awareness

Consciousness

Bliss

Heart

Center

Limitless

Light

Immortal

Infinite

Joy

Unity

Pure

Unconditional

Satisfaction

Absolute

Truth

One

Mercy

Delight

Peace

Wisdom

Over the years I have had other opportunities to do this exercise and each time it emerges with a new perspective and evolution. Here are two of the latest versions:

I AM divine.

I AM a brilliant star and light

I AM called

I AM being and becoming

I AM the ocean, vast and calling me to greatness

I AM creative and creating my identity

I AM a caregiver, caring for caregivers

I AM a trusted advisor and friend

I AM an excellent trainer

I AM a giver

I AM ascending

I am Lani Almanza and my mission is to bring health, wealth, and wellness to the world. My unique gift is that I have an amazing ability to touch hearts with patience and kindness. My most valuable talent is that I am a trusted advisor, teacher, trainer, and mentor in showing others how to live a more activated life. My commitment to you is that I will be your guide to the resources you need to achieve wellness today.

In writing this I am also called to speak about humility, ha‘aha‘a, which to me is different from being or acting humble. Humility speaks to a philosophy of openness and inclusion. It is an effort to step forward in respect and honor, not in any way that is prideful or arrogant. We can acknowledge our successes and achievements in and with humility when they serve to uplift others.

Reflection: If you haven't done this before, or lately, take a moment now and create your list for "I..." and see where it takes you.

"The purpose of life is to create your Self anew, in the grandest version of the greatest vision you ever had about who you are." ~ Neale Donald Walsch

Begin the living of it by declaring it!

Evolve

> To change or develop slowly, often into a better, more complex, or more advanced state.
>
> To come forth gradually into being

A prominent theme in this book has been transformation and the sometimes painful process it can be. The word EVOLVE has shifted my perspective. Whether it be in our personal or professional lives, our journey must be one of evolving - of moving to that better place. If we look at the theory of evolution, what doesn't evolve becomes extinct. It is a word with motion and intent to move forward and upward. Not just better but advanced. For me that has been the process of moving from a doing perspective and lifestyle to one of being. In being—more mindful, aware, conscious, deliberate, motivated, and loving. This is not to say that it is any less challenging than a transformation, but I think the difference is in the intent. Evolve seems to carry a different energy and may take us into different and challenging circumstances, but always with a purpose to grow and improve.

"She remembered who she was and the game changed." ~ Layla Delia

Leaving Tracks

"We will be known forever by the tracks we leave." ~ Native American Dakota Proverb

---

How should I end the book? I pondered this question for some time and it came to me that there isn't an end. Or at least I hope there is no end. I hope that wherever you are on your personal journey, there is something here that has helped you reflect on both where you have been and where you are going. We are all climbing the same mountain and at every point along the way have a new view and perspective of what has passed and what might lay ahead. Each step offers us a new choice on how to proceed. Yes, there will be obstacles and challenges, but also triumphs and victories, and my hope is that in some small way I have made the journey a little easier for you. Choose health and happiness, but most of all choose love and leave your own tracks for those who follow.

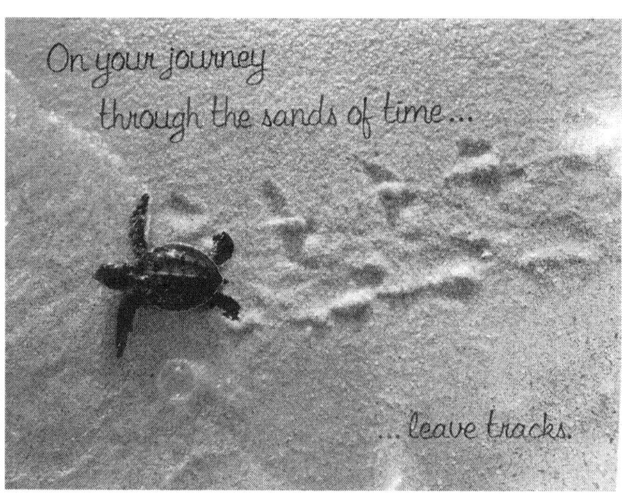

On your journey
through the sands of time...
...leave tracks.

Epilogue

I want the reader to understand there is someone like them, who has shared life experiences, and through my journey they can find useful resources towards a healthier and happier life. I want the reader to have a feeling that there is someone to walk alongside them offering the wisdom of having walked the path before. I also want the reader to be able to connect with the true meaning of ALOHA and use it as a guide as they move between doing and being.

As we continue our journey together, I want to share one more lesson in ALOHA with you. The year that Jacob transitioned, I had begun working for the American Cancer Society and moved through different roles of leadership over my tenure there. About four years into my career there I was confronted by a very disgruntled and disturbed volunteer. She felt she had been slighted and intended to drag my name through the mud. She contacted my supervisor and when she didn't get the response she felt entitled to, took it all the way up the corporate chain to the CEO. Even with a personal apology, she threatened to "go public" with this perceived transgression attacking my integrity in the community. It really started to get to me and then I received affirmations from colleagues, friends and family that my integrity was built on a firm foundation. The one that I cherish to this day was from my husband who wrote:

"What is:

- *35 years of marriage*
- *Raised four children*

- *Transformed by the youngest child*
- *Grandmother to two angels*
- *Makes a living helping the frightened and helpless*

I can't imagine an annoyance that could blemish this large life. Because nothing can change what is."

When I look back on this now, what occurs to me is that it felt so personal because I was now discovering how to be my authentic self and what my core values were in the face of this experience. I was both angry and hurt, but having done all I could to take any responsibility, I eventually came to the understanding that it really wasn't about me and with the affirmations I received I was able to let go and move forward with ALOHA in my own integrity and authenticity.

It is my hope that as you walked alongside me on this journey, and through this book, I have done what I set out to do. That you have found an alaka'i, who is leading with ALOHA, that has paved the way so that your journey can be easier, healthier, and more fulfilled.

What Will Matter, by Michael Josephson

Ready or not, some day it will all come to an end.

There will be no more sunrises, no minutes, hours or days.

All the things you collected, whether treasured or forgotten, will pass to someone else.

Your wealth, fame and temporal power will shrivel to irrelevance.

It will not matter what you owned or what you were owed.

Your grudges, resentments, frustrations and jealousies will finally disappear.

So too, your hopes, ambitions, plans and to-do lists will expire.

The wins and losses that once seemed so important will fade away.

It won't matter where you came from or what side of the tracks you lived on at the end.

Even your gender and skin color will be irrelevant.

So, what will matter? How will the value of your days be measured?

What will matter is not what you bought but what you built, not what you got but what you gave.

What will matter is not your success but your significance.

What will matter is not what you learned but what you taught.

What will matter is every act of integrity, compassion, courage or sacrifice that enriched, empowered or encouraged others to emulate your example.

What will matter is not your competence but your character.

What will matter is not how many people you knew, but how many will feel a lasting loss when you're gone.

What will matter is not your memories but the memories of those who loved you.

What will matter is how long you will be remembered, by whom and for what.

Living a life that matters doesn't happen by accident.

It's not a matter of circumstance but of choice.

Choose to live a life that matters.

Acknowledgements

First and foremost, to my family, without whom much of this story would not have been written. To lifelong friends who are woven into my life journey, LL*, JR*, LC*, AC*. To my mentors and Alaka'i - CT*, MR*, and AP* who continue to inspire me from their eternal realm. To those who encouraged my writing; Maryann Wassel, my 9th grade English teacher who became friend and mentor; Lorna Hershinow a college writing professor who told me I was a good writer; and Elizabeth Kunimoto another college professor who said the Status Report 2003 paper would be a chapter of a book I would write. To Meriam Boldewijn whose own caregiver story, in her own voice, gave me the courage to begin my book and who introduced me to Sarah Jefferis, my amazingly intuitive writing coach. To L Ānuenue Pūnua for her expertise in Hawaiian language and her editing. To Cindy Wells Klingberg for her exceptional graphic art talents in creating the cover art. To Erin Moncada, Kirk D'Amico, and Anne Moriarty for saying yes to proofread and review, you were selected with much gratitude and aloha for the imprint you have had on my life. I know there are many more who have walked with me or have had an influence in my journey who deserve thanks as well - so with much ALOHA I say thank you.

Appendixes

References*

Auntie Pilahi Paki.pdf

https://static1.squarespace.com/static/57d3705203596e4e5be15d77/t/5a253d468165f55746ea1870/1512389958588/Aloha+by+Auntie+Pilahi+Paki.pdf

Blue Zones Power-9

https://www.bluezones.com/2016/11/power-9/

Hawaiian Naming Traditions

https://keolamagazine.com/culture/hawaiian-naming-traditions/

Attitudinal Healing

* https://www.ahinternational.org/about/the-twelve-principles-of-ah/

Book list

Conversations with God, Book 3, Neale Donald Walsch, 1998

Ikigai, The Japanese Secret to a Long and Happy Life, Hector Garcia & Frances Mirales, 2016

Manufacturing Consent, Noam Chomsky & Edward S. Herman, 1988

Time Management from the Inside Out, Julie Morgenstern, 2000

Simple Abundance, Sarah Ban Breathnach, 1995

The Anatomy of Hope, Jerome Groopman, 2004

The Grief Recovery Handbook, John W. James, 2009

The Simple Abundance Journal of Gratitude, Sarah Ban Breathnach, 1996

The Year of Magical Thinking, Joan Didion, 2005

The 5 Second Rule, Mel Robbins, 2017

The High Five Habit, Mel Robbins, 2021

The E Myth, Michael Gerber, 1998

Thrive, The Third Metric to Redefining Success and Creating a Life of Well-Being, Wisdom, and Wonder. Arianna Huffington, 2014, Christabella, LLC

For more resources, workshops and private consulting go to www.alakaiassociates.com

Made in the USA
Columbia, SC
24 September 2024